Praise for *Going to Ground*

"A sweet little book . . . there are real pleasures to be had. Blackmarr's voice is by turns pert and engaging, musing and meditative. . . . [This book] gives us the warmth of Amy Blackmarr's friendship, and the remarkable gift of watching her come to know herself."
  —*The Washington Post*

"Lovely . . . Blackmarr finishes her pieces with understatement rather than fanfare. That keeps the electricity humming. And when she reaches for some universal truth she does it with a dart throw."
  —*Chicago Tribune*

"Three cheers for Amy Blackmarr's *Going to Ground*. It's wise, true, and unfailingly interesting. I can't wait to start giving it as must-read gifts to my friends."
  —Mary Hood, author of *How Far She Went* and *Familiar Heat*

"[Blackmarr's] tendency to understate seems remarkably refreshing in this era of loud, obtuse moral posturing. Her feminine perspective offers a welcome counterpoint to Thoreau's, and her clear-eyed take on nature (both human and earthy) proves optimistic and well-written. *Going to Ground* is the kind of book that offers solace from the world by leading us back into it."
  —*Arkansas Times*

"A delightful book. Amy Blackmarr's voice is at once strong, full of humor, grief, spunk, and charm. Sit down on a front porch step with a steaming cup of coffee, relax, and savor each page of *Going to Ground*."
  —Mary Swander, author of *Out of this World*

"Not only is this a sumptuous collection of personal essays, it provides escapism for those who choose to live in the outdoors vicariously, as well as an inspiration to others to pursue a dream."
    —*Lexington Herald-Leader*

"Blackmarr negotiates quite humbly the tricky line between self-reliance and self-congratulation. *Going to Ground* details an examined life close to the soil, the first and last condition of existence: Life springs from the ground and dies into it as well. And the beauty is that the girl who died into becoming a woman is still grounded in the woman herself."
    —*Arkansas Democrat-Gazette*

"The life may be 'simple' at Amy Blackmarr's South Georgia pond, but her compelling voice is rich and nuanced. This postmodern *Walden* experience is alive with winning characters and the kind of thinking that only comes from living quietly enough to follow the twisting trail of fresh perception. Each chapter rings with insight."
    —Patricia Hampl, author of *Virgin Time* and *A Romantic Education*

"Blackmarr's descriptions of the landscape, weather, flora, and fauna take readers on a journey to a quiet place."
    —*The Daily Sentinel*

"Elegant . . . the graceful pieces are imbued with a sense of calm and delight in nature."
    —*Publishers Weekly*

"A graceful descent into the Thoreauvian life of mind and nature . . . Readers are likely to hear this as a welcome invocation, and to fall effortlessly under the entrancing spell of her words."
    —*Kirkus Reviews*

"Captivating . . . For all those readers who can't return to a solitary life, *Going to Ground* is the next best thing."
    —*Booklist*

PENGUIN BOOKS

GOING TO GROUND

Amy Blackmarr grew up in Georgia, but lived in Kansas for twelve years before returning home to the family farm to write. Her essays are broadcast on "Georgia Gazette," a weekly features show on the Peach State Public Radio Network, as well as "Up to Date," a weekly news show on Kansas City's NPR affiliate. A Self Fellow at the University of Kansas, she lives in a tree house outside of Lawrence, Kansas.

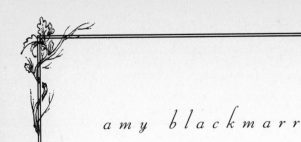

amy blackmarr

GOING TO GROUND

Simple Life on a Georgia Pond

PENGUIN BOOKS

PENGUIN BOOKS
Published by the Penguin Group
Penguin Putnam Inc., 375 Hudson Street,
New York, New York 10014, U.S.A.
Penguin Books Ltd, 27 Wrights Lane,
London W8 5TZ, England
Penguin Books Australia Ltd, Ringwood,
Victoria, Australia
Penguin Books Canada Ltd, 10 Alcorn Avenue,
Toronto, Ontario, Canada M4V 3B2
Penguin Books (N.Z.) Ltd, 182–190 Wairau Road,
Auckland 10, New Zealand

Penguin Books Ltd, Registered Offices:
Harmondsworth, Middlesex, England

First published in the United States of America by Viking Penguin,
a member of Penguin Putnam Inc. 1997
Published in Penguin Books 1998

1   3   5   7   9   10   8   6   4   2

Grateful acknowledgment is made for permission to reprint "Tea is nought
but this" by Sen Rikyu from *Tea Life, Tea Mind* by Soshitsu Sen XV.
By permission of Weatherhill, Inc.

Some of the essays in this book, in part and in different form, appeared in
the *Spectator*, Valdosta State University, Valdosta, Georgia and in *Pegasus*,
Abraham Baldwin College, Tifton, Georgia.

Earlier versions of these selections won the nonfiction competition at Augusta
College's 1995 Sandhills Writers' Conference, Augusta, Georgia. "Different Light"
placed second in the Greater Augusta Arts Council's 1995 Porter Fleming
Writing Competition. Portions of these essays have been
broadcasted on Peach State Public Radio.

THE LIBRARY OF CONGRESS HAS CATALOGUED THE HARDCOVER AS FOLLOWS:
Blackmarr, Amy.
Going to ground: simple life on a Georgia pond / Amy Blackmarr.
p.   cm.
ISBN 0-670-87567-8 (hc.)
ISBN 0 14 02.6692 5 (pbk.)
1. Country life—Georgia—Lax.   2. Blackmarr, Amy.   3. Lax (Ga.)—Biography.
4. Natural History—Georgia—Lax.   I. Title.
F294.L25B58   1997
975.8'823—dc21   97–9471

Printed in the United States of America
Set in Centaur
Designed by Judith Abbate

To Joe Stofiel

Special thanks to Mom, Kelly, Uncle Burns,
my best friend, Deborah G. Smith,
Joshua McKinney, Nick Taylor,
and the English faculty of Valdosta State University

The Man who cannot wonder, who does not habitually wonder, is but a Pair of Spectacles behind which there is no Eye.

THOMAS   CARLYLE

CONTENTS

PROLOGUE

what gave

$\mathscr{I}$ turned thirty-three the year I decided to sell the paralegal business in Kansas I had owned for eight years and move back home to South Georgia, where I grew up. I'd been sitting in the chair in my office, staring absently at my computer screen, waiting for motivation, when it struck me that this office was not where I wanted to be, that this work was not what I wanted to do with my life—and that thirty years later I did not want to wake up regretting, like so many people I knew, that I had never opened that dance studio when I had the chance, never driven to Alaska for the summer, never become an archaeologist or an astronaut or a poet, never finished school, never divorced, never married, never had children, never not had children, never joined the Peace Corps, never learned Spanish, never bought that fishing boat on the Florida Gulf and made myself a permanent bed in the cabin.

Or, in my case, never having written. But I was like Hawthorne: I could not work at the office and write, too. For me, it had to be one or the other.

Coming back home was easier for me than it might have been. Our family farm near Lax, Georgia, was ten miles from Ocilla, my hometown, and I had always harbored a desire to live in my grandfather's old fishing cabin there beside one of the farm's three ponds. Too, I had often nursed monastic inclinations and loved the idea of a rustic lifestyle more conducive to contemplation than my city apartment (or so I believed), so the rural beauty and seclusion of the farm was compelling. An equally strong attraction was that my grandmother, whom I deeply loved, had reached her nineties, and I saw the move as an opportunity to spend time with her. That I knew a woman in Kansas who wanted to buy my business was added incentive.

Eight months after I made the decision to leave Kansas, I moved in at the cabin in Lax. That was October. It rained all the way through to January and we were twenty-one inches above normal by the end of the year. But I had a space heater and long underwear, a library card, my computer, an idea for a novel, a prayer rug, a big red four-wheel-drive Dodge Dakota pickup, and enough money to get by for a while. I was happy.

In November, my family moved my grandmother— we called her MaRe, pronounced Ma-Ree for Mama Reba—to the Americus, Georgia, Magnolia Manor, a dignified place for the elderly and the infirm built and funded by the Methodists. Every Saturday morning, I locked the cabin door, closed the red gates that stood at each end of the winding quarter-mile drive through the pines to the paved road, and tooled off to Americus to spend the day with her. There, I steered her around the aisles at Wal-Mart in the guest wheelchair while she directed me to the Depends, the Oil of Olay, and the Kleenexes. We ate baked potatoes at Wendy's and bought Ritz Bits crackers to replenish her always dwindling supply. Then we washed her clothes and tidied her room, and after supper we played bingo in the game room with her friends before I headed back to Lax.

When MaRe came home at Christmas, I brought her out to the pond, and we sat by the bank and watched the turtles and talked about my grandfather. He had loved this place, and MaRe and I had spent many days out here together when I was a girl, bream-fishing from the banks with our cane poles and crickets and red-and-white plastic bobbers, and having picnics and parties.

During our conversation that December day, MaRe told me that she wanted to keep this part of the farm—the pond, the cabin, the surrounding pines—in the family, even if the rest were sold. She would tell her son, she said. She remarked how happy the birds seemed at the pond—they were loud that day—and then a breeze came up and she got cold, and we left. Two months later she was diagnosed with breast cancer. The following December, she died. Her children immediately put the farm up for sale. I doubted MaRe had ever told them of her wish to keep the pond.

Going to Ground is therefore a journey of place. It is not a continuous narrative, but rather a collection of essays linked simply by my notion to write them here, at the cabin, where for five years I have had the privilege of getting to know home again. Nevertheless, contrary to my expectation, the nature of the experiences that these pieces recount, explore, examine, extends far beyond the boundaries that enclose these particular five years. Life, I have discovered, is not a continuous narrative, so much as a grab bag of scenes played and then replayed as the moment I occupy recalls them and brings them into focus. I continually comprehend them, and they continually evolve, and their relevance is fluid and will not stay still under the sharp spotlight of my eyes and mind but alters constantly, like a pond that possesses no color of its own but can only mirror the sky and the change of light through which I see it. And what meaning might become apparent at any single instant can lift as easily as a heron and glide as silently through a white summer sky and disappear as completely into what lies beyond my vision. What can be found here, then, is less narrative than scene, less word than image—less explanation than experience, which is the only certainty I know.

Amy Blackmarr
Lax, Georgia
June 1996

GOING TO GROUND

Simple Life on a Georgia Pond

cave·dweller

You must come with no intentions of discovery.

BARRY LOPEZ

I was standing at the cabin window in an August heat wave near sunset, watching my hard-bodied little gray dog Max dig in his cave. I had given up filling it in. Now the concrete blocks I had patched the hole with last summer hung suspended in the cave's earth ceiling, threatening to smother Max in a late-summer rain. My German shepherd, Queenie, stood at the edge of the hole peering in, the way she peers in from the edge of everything Max does.

Max had so far managed a depth of about four feet over as many months, on the east side of the cabin where the dirt is hard-packed because it hasn't been dug since the building was moved out here four decades ago. Max was so deep down in his cave that only his back end was visible, vibrating as he pawed furiously at the dirt, his tail tucked under, not stuck straight up in midair like a lightning rod, its usual position. Sometimes he would back out of the cave, snarl and snap at Queenie, and stand panting until he caught his breath; then he'd disappear again to dig some more. He kept at this task for a long time. I watched until it grew too dark for me to see.

My cousin and I used to steal my grandmother's silver tablespoons out of the kitchen drawer and dig to China in the driveway. After we'd scooped out an inch or two of dirt, my cousin would put her ear to the hole and swear she could hear people speaking Chinese on the other side. She swore on the Bible. My cousin was older and her daddy was a preacher, so I believed her. So when I put my ear to the hole I could hear Chinese people, too, and I yelled at them in English and imagined they could hear me. I put my feet into the hole and imagined going down, down, down, until I popped out on the far side of the world, where all the women wore silk dresses and all the dogs had pug noses. I knew this because I read library books.

I told a friend this story once, so now when she comes out to the cabin she goes to the edge of Max's cave and folds her arms and bows. Then she looks at me and grins.

I have this other friend who peers into Max's cave and shakes her head. "I am in awe," she says. "This cave-building is so doglike." She keeps all her dogs indoors.

My mother is afraid I'll fall into the cave or that a rattlesnake will crawl in and take over.

At my grandmother's house when I was five, I used to sit on the floor in front of the television inside an unbroken circle of magazines and Sears and JC Penney catalogues. Nobody could come inside the circle unless I opened the invisible door.

When I turned nine, I made a secret tunnel through long stands of bamboo that grew in a vacant lot next to our yard. At the end of the tunnel, I cleared a round space to sit in and blocked the entrance with a barrier of pink and white camellias that I stole from the neighbors' bushes all over the block.

When I was sixteen, I turned my Gordon Lightfoot tape up loud in my Cutlass Supreme and drove out fast to the country, enclosed in guitar and song and the sweet-earth smell of dug peanuts in the fields of rural South Georgia.

All the way through my twenties I was married.

Now I live in a fishing cabin way back in the pines with two dogs and two cats and innumerable wild things. My nearest neighbors, Gene and Alice, are half a mile down the road and I don't get much company. If strangers come to the gate, I let the dogs snarl and snap them away, while I gaze at pictures of johnboat, blue heron, armadillo, and pine, wringing out story.

I like to flatter myself that I live something like Thoreau did. I didn't build this place with my own hands and I don't have nine bean rows—although I did have a garden once until the fire ants ate it. But there is a bee-loud glade nearby where Gene lets a friend raise honey and out-side my cabin door is a seven-acre pond, and the land has a wide character.

This tin-roofed, tarpapered shack has character, too, even if it isn't insulated. In the 1920s it was the commissary at my great-grandfather's lumberyard in Ocilla, where I grew up. My grandfather—we called him Pop—moved the place out here to Lax in the fifties, to the farm my great-grandfather had left him. Pop dragged the building up the hill through the cow pasture, set it down facing the pond he'd made by damming a thin creek that rambled half a mile westward to the Willacoochee River, and had himself a fishing cabin. He put the outhouse in back, inside a stand of live oaks.

Later on, when the trains stopped coming through Ocilla, MaRe got some men to take apart the oak ticket counter at the train depot and bring it out to the pond. They had to put it back together again inside the cabin because it was two feet too wide to come through the door. Now it divides the kitchen from the rest of the house. MaRe pasted over its shelves with orange paisley paper and painted the rest of the thing green. Yet it bears reminders of that older time. A "Drink Coca-Cola" bottle opener is still screwed to one end, and century-old glue still holds the original leather cover to the countertop.

MaRe painted many things green, in indescribable shades between pale grass and English peas. She painted the concrete blocks green in the closet, and the kitchen cabinets and the bookcases and the curtain rods and the window frames and all the inside walls of her house in town. But she left the cabin's plywood paneling its original medium brown and hung fishnets decorated with ceramic angelfish and Creepy Crawler frogs behind the green vinyl sofa and the blue vinyl chair. Then with characteristic *joie de vivre* she brought out the orange curtains and the yellow Formica dining room table with chrome legs. And the green dinner plates shaped like large-mouth bass.

So altogether the cabin was never the height of aesthetic refinement, but its relative comfort sufficed for fishermen, fisherwomen, and fisherchildren. Pop drove out here every night after work, to hammer and nail and shoot at the squirrels and nip at his bottle of Canadian Club. Later, he tore down the outhouse and added an indoor bathroom and a second room, and MaRe had the garden club and the book club and the Baptist Women's Missionary Union out for luncheons. I had birthday parties with bamboo poles for favors.

Then one day Pop died. MaRe got old and I moved away and, except for old Johnny, who mowed the yard and brought his family to sit on the banks and fish, people stopped coming. Until I came back five years ago, the mice and the squirrels were very happy here inside the sofa cushions and under the rope rug.

*N*ow the green and blue vinyl furniture is gone, replaced with the rattan I brought from the city, and the mice have moved into new nests behind the paneling. And naturally I've had to patch a few things. One November afternoon a gust of wind blasted a windowpane out of its green frame and rain began to blow into the back of my computer. I went outside in the lightning and stuck the window together with glass tape. It's still holding.

By spring the bathroom ceiling was leaking, so I climbed up on the roof and filled the hole with plumber's putty.

I bought a roll of hail screen to cover the places where the squirrels had chewed through the tarpaper, but I couldn't get the staples to hold. When I pulled at the tarpaper, it went to pieces in my hands—except where the dirtdobber nests held it together from underneath. But the walls hadn't started to rot yet, so I let the tarpaper alone and twist-tied the hail screen to a gap in the fence where a pine tree had crashed down on it in the middle of the night.

When winter comes I jam pieces of two-by-four into the spaces under the eaves to keep out the squirrels and stuff T-shirts into the cracks around the ledges to keep out the cold. I can't keep the mice out. They have secret entrances.

The wood floor humps up in summer and sinks in winter and it's going soft in places. One day when the weather is cold I'll get up the nerve to crawl under the cabin among the rattlesnake nests and figure out how to shore up the floor. Until then, I don't step everywhere.

Also, the back half of the cabin has sunk about ten inches, so it's a pretty good slide down those seventeen feet from the back door to the north wall. This wouldn't be a problem except that when company sits on one end of the sofa, the other end flies up like a seesaw. But I can't do anything about that.

Contrary to what I believed when I came back to this place, the road of my discovery was not limited to the geography of my home soil—Samuel Johnson said the truth is wherever you are. I walk now breathless all the narrow turnings of this new cave I inhabit, following the drawings I dare myself to see, and find myself returned down every path of my existence. But being here, inside this wide space of whispered quiet and watching, has given my pictures time to open out, move, unfold into honeysuckle vines, water oaks, rust-colored September grasses, and living creatures of light and shadow that I can comprehend.

Out here an aluminum ladder stands propped against the cabin beside the croquet set with colored balls my cousins and I played with as children, and a rake, a shovel, and a hoe lie across the rotting racks where we once kept the fishing poles. A wheelbarrow has lain upside down beneath the live oak by the bathroom window for as long as I can remember. On the west end of the yard, a beaten johnboat leans against a pine, its anchor a concrete block tied to a rope. From early spring to midsummer, pink and white blossoms spill into the water from the blueberry bushes and dogwoods my grandmother planted along the banks of the pond. A cast-iron sign that once hung on the back gate to welcome guests now lies on the concrete ledge by the cabin door, the thin dark space behind it making a shaded niche for green anoles and blue-tailed skinks. "Who passes through this friendly gate comes neither too early nor stays too late," the sign says.

These are the pictographs my life has drawn around me. I came back home intending to discover them, decipher them; but what I saw with my intention was not, it turned out, what was true. What emerged from beyond my vision as it wrote itself into story, was. Holding out my expectation for something familiar, I watched my pictures move and reshape themselves and, like an ancient hand sketches tribal myth in charcoal along a cavern wall, in the telling, stories I had never known came quietly clear. Now, I draw them into memory.

the voice of fancy

Samuel Taylor Coleridge wrote that fancy takes the materials at hand and plays them into patterns—like poetry, song, story. MaRe was a drama coach in the early 1920s. Sponsored by the Wayne P. Sewell Producing Company, she traveled all over the Southeast by rail, putting on plays and musicals in small towns from Alabama to the Carolinas, Tennessee to Florida. She didn't travel with an acting troupe but held tryouts in the towns, so the local talent performed the shows she directed along with, sometimes, herself. MaRe could sing, dance, act, and elocute, and she was youthful and independent and the gentlemen were so infatuated with her that sometimes they followed her from town to town. A few of these asked her to marry them. Pop was the one she accepted.

MaRe loved Longfellow and James Whitcomb Riley, and in 1916 when Riley died she acquired the ten-volume memorial edition of his works, "Including Poems and Prose Sketches, many of which have not heretofore been published; an authentic Biography, an elaborate Index and numerous Illustrations in color." She must have carried the volumes with her on her travels, for crammed within their pages are one-act play scripts, newspaper clippings of poems she liked, advertisements for guides on "economy in stagecraft," even penciled accountings of her expenses for train tickets and meals. Inside the cover of volume five, she wrote the page number for "Little Orphant Annie," which she could recite from memory with remarkable feeling all the ninety-three years of her life. On Halloween nights when my cousins and I were children we loved to listen to the rise and fall of her voice as she chanted Riley's verse:

> *An' all us other childern, when the supper-things*
> *is done,*
> *We set around the kitchen fire an' has the mostest*
> *fun*
> *A-list'nin' to the witch-tales 'at Annie tells*
> *about,*
> *An' the Gobble-uns 'at gits you*
> *Ef you*
> *Don't*
> *Watch*
> *Out!*

MaRe told her five granddaughters how our little shadows went in and out with us, that little boys were made of puppydog tails, and how the teeny-tiny woman lost her teeny-tiny teakettle lid. She told us about an old woman who lived in a shoe with too many children. We learned that billy goats gruff couldn't go *trap trap trap!* across the bridge because the troll would eat them and that we could climb a beanstalk to the sky if we weren't afraid of the giant who lived there. She told us about the mermaids who lived in crystal castles under the sea. When I spent the night with her, she spun bedtime stories of fairies and princesses and magical jeweled boxes and the boy she called Poor Little Johnny, who lived with his mother and his cruel father in a cottage in the woods and never had enough to eat. "Once upon a time, Poor Little Johnny . . ." she would begin, and off my imagination would go, trailing down dark wooded paths after lost children, knocking at the kitchen doors of black-hatted, long-fingered witches who poked the stomachs of little boys to see how fat they were.

After MaRe moved to the Magnolia Manor, on Saturdays she'd leave her door ajar for me. The door opened into a tiny hall that led past the bathroom into her single small room.

One morning I stepped inside the partly open door and, as usual, called to her to let her know I was there so I wouldn't startle her when I walked in. "MaRe?" I said. "I'm here."

She didn't answer.

I pushed the door open wider and called again. "MaRe?"

Still she didn't answer. I glanced around the bathroom, but it was empty, and I could hear no noise from the bedroom.

Mildly concerned—MaRe was always waiting for me when I arrived—I decided to go on in. She had been diagnosed with breast cancer at ninety-two and had undergone a mastectomy and radiation therapy. Now, at ninety-three and with heart problems, she was weakening steadily. My mind raced with possibilities as I paused in the hall, preparing to enter her room.

But at last I took a breath, and just as I started forward, MaRe popped out from behind the door. "Peep-eyeeee!" she cried, and burst out laughing.

$\mathcal{I}$ drove my red pickup truck for a year after I moved to the cabin. MaRe didn't have the strength to lift herself into it, so I kept concrete blocks in the bed to use for steps. After eating lunch one day we were walking back to the truck when some people driving by stopped to ask directions. I stayed to talk, and MaRe went on. A few minutes later when I turned around, I was astonished to see MaRe's head sticking up above the roof of the cab. As soon as she saw me looking, her eyes widened and she started to holler. "Amy! Come help me! Hurry up!" she said.

I ran around to the passenger side of the truck and found her spread across the open doorway like Spider Woman, clutching the roof with the tips of her fingers and the edge of the floor with her toes. She had tried to climb in from the curb without waiting for the steps. She was a little under five feet tall then and less than ninety pounds, and not really frail, but fragile. I pried her loose and managed to get her into the seat without breaking her.

"Phew!" she said. "I was really stuck."

"Why didn't you call me sooner?" I asked.

"I couldn't get my breath!" she said. "I was laughing too hard!"

$\mathcal{N}$ow a small silver-framed photograph of MaRe sits before me on top of my computer, just beneath the screen. She is holding her hand to her mouth, covering a laugh. Beside the picture is a Chinese mudman who toasts the sky with a cup of tea. The two of them—MaRe and the mudman—hold court with five fat cast-iron frogs, whose sizes range downward from the length of half my thumb to the tip of my little finger. Each sits hunched behind the other, ready to spring. My mother gave me the frogs at Christmas in a fit of laughter. She had wrapped each one in tissue paper inside a single box, and the smaller they got as they tumbled from their wrappings, the harder she laughed.

Behind the frogs stands a miniature wooden chair covered in dried flowers, another present from my mother—for the Muses, she said. A brown rock with sparkles of mica lies at the foot of the chair, next to a flat red stone etched with gray lines, a chunk of crystal, a round orange stone, a broken flint spear point, two slivers of sweet gum gnawed by beavers, a stack of Audubon field guides on reptiles, wildflowers, trees, and birds, a paperback thesaurus, and a dictionary. Nearby, a stick of copal incense is burning, and a mug of steaming coffee keeps my fingers warm, the space heater behind me having raised the cabin temperature to just under sixty. Outside the window, the day is clear. Earlier I saw a belted kingfisher on the fence post by the west gate, and now the crows are cawing on the far side of the pond. Light glitters on the water, catching on the wet backs of turtles and in the feathery tops of the pale, tall grasses around the banks. The dogs sleep in the sun. I sit at MaRe's yellow Formica and chrome dining room table and play pictures into patterns, and I am my grandmother's voice.

the faces of perception

I once drove past a wagon train on the south side of Willacoochee: it was lumbering over the stretches of bridge that cross the riverbed. I was on the way to the doctor in Valdosta. As I came flying around a curve in my new Geo Metro at seventy miles an hour, I was brought up short by a highway department vehicle trundling along the side of the road, bearing a fluorescent orange sign. "WAGON TRAIN AHEAD," the sign said.

Oh, sure, I thought, and kept going.

But soon I saw a dozen broad-shouldered, rough-looking men on horses. One of them held the line across the road before the bridges, and when he saw my tiny green car barreling toward him he thrust his gloved palm at me. I stopped. This cowboy wore a white felt hat and a red bandanna around his neck and a dark duster on this the coldest day I could recall for a December. I thought him peculiar; I thought the whole thing peculiar. Watching him made me think of the years I'd spent in Kansas before I moved back to the South, and long drives through the Flint Hills in the western half of the state, where to my mind's eye the Indians still wore war paint and rode spirited horses along the bluffs. This fellow in front of me with his spurs and his muscled, nimble-limbed bay was out of context in Willacoochee, Georgia. He belonged to Dodge City or Abilene. He probably had a name out of *Lonesome Dove*. Augustus. Call. Pea Eye.

I could see behind him, where the other cowboys had ridden up beside four covered wagons drawn by mules that were making their laborious way across the bridges. The wagons were loaded with people—as well as, I presumed, camping gear. I couldn't imagine this bunch tying their stock up to wrought-iron motel room railings at sundown, agreeing to meet at dawn for breakfast at Shoney's.

After the wagons crossed the bridges, the mules pulled them onto the side of the road and I and all the other startled drivers who had piled up behind me crawled past them in our motorized vehicles and tried not to stare. I zoomed on to the doctor in Valdosta, a wizened little man with birdlike eyes, a bow tie, and a sharp tongue. I was complaining about stress, which I believed was causing my outbreak of atopic dermatitis.

"Mumbo jumbo," he said. "I don't believe any of it."

I bristled. "But it seems like I only have these problems when—" I said. "Everything I've read says that stress—"

"Hell. You don't have any idea what stress is," he snapped. "You people today think you're having stress when the television goes on the blink. I'll tell you what stress is. Stress is getting up at daylight and heading west to the frontier in a covered wagon. *That's* stress."

I didn't tell him about the Willacoochee wagon train. He would have thought I was making it up.

*O*n the way back home I passed the procession again. They'd gone about twenty miles. An old woman in one of the wagons had fallen asleep. Her head bobbed as I drove by.

*S*ometimes for me the lines between fancy and reality blur and I wonder if I've witnessed a kind of cosmic slip, maybe seen things from the other side of the looking glass. When I take the boat out on the pond on a still day, I wonder sometimes which face is real: the one slightly sunburned, with the chapped lips and blue eyes—or the one in the water, superimposed on reflections of tree and sky, set moving by water bugs or minnows or the tip of my fishing pole. Perhaps what is real is beyond the definable. Emerson suggested that the world exists only as a revelation of the mind. "Build, therefore, your own world," he said.

I once saw a man emerge from the same room twice. He came out of the room, greeted me, and crossed the hall to get a Coke. A few seconds later, as I headed for the room he had left, he came out of it again, greeted me anew, and crossed the hall. I stopped and thought about it, but I couldn't get what I'd seen to make sense. So then I wondered whether I'd really seen it.

Years later, I decided that I had seen it, one night when I woke up and saw my body lying in bed next to me. I lay there for a long while in a mild panic, examining my profile, trying to get myself back together. I couldn't do it. So I went back to sleep, hoping that when I awoke the next morning I'd be whole again. I was—but I've never forgotten.

When I was sixteen, three years after Pop died, I was out here at the cabin one night, sitting on the sofa with a boyfriend, when we heard someone pacing back and forth across the roof—not the sloped tin roof on the old part of the cabin, but the flat tar roof that covers the newer half. It sounded like someone walking on a gravel road in street shoes. We raced home and told MaRe. She laughed. She said it was probably Pop, trying to find out what we were doing.

A year before old Johnny passed away, I saw him in the grocery store one day, and he told me that MaRe had come to see him on the December morning she died. She was bedridden ninety miles away in Americus, but still she came, he said, and asked him to mow the lawn at her house in town because she was expecting company there. So the lawn was mowed and the hedges were trimmed long before the people started arriving with the food. "I see her three, four times since then," Johnny said.

"Why doesn't she come to see me?" I asked him.

"She afraid she scare you," he said.

My friend Larry Lott used to tell me ghost stories about the house trailer he lived in. His mother confirmed them, so I believed they were true. I was sitting on the sofa in Lott's trailer one evening around suppertime, facing the front door, waiting for him to get home from work so we could go to Brushy Creek Cemetery. We often went out to Brushy Creek at midnight, to sit with our backs against the gravestones and watch for revenants.

Lott's mother was in the kitchen. Suddenly I heard the lock turn in the door, and I heard the door open and close. I heard footsteps pass the sofa where I was sitting and disappear down the hall. But the door had never opened and I'd never seen a thing.

I took my first vacation alone when I was twenty-nine. I wanted to learn how to travel by myself, become comfortable eating alone in strange restaurants, carry my own luggage, rent a car, check into a hotel room. I did myself the favor, however, of choosing a destination I already knew well. I went to the west coast of Florida, where I had spent many childhood summers, and where my cousin lived.

My cousin was the sun-browned, silver-haired, blue-eyed captain of his own twenty-eight-foot yacht. He sailed me out into the Gulf with a handful of his friends one day, on the way to an island known for its wide white unpopulated beaches and an abundance of sand dollars. En route to the island, we sailed by a motorboat whose occupants were playing with a dolphin. I watched, fascinated, as the animal played in the water, chattering, leaping up to take things offered by fingers, gliding along the side of the motorboat within easy reach of hands that stretched forward to rub the top of his head.

Eventually, though, I heard the engine roar as the motorboat surged ahead. The people waved at the dolphin as the boat sped away. And the dolphin, the wild dolphin, leapt high into the air, much higher than before, and performed a perfect backflip. When I mentioned to the woman standing near me how surprised I was to see a dolphin do a backflip in the wild like that, to see a wild dolphin so friendly, she shrugged. "I've seen a lot of dolphins," she said, and asked me if I cared for another glass of wine. I shrugged and said yes.

Earlier on that same trip, as the plane flew over Tampa Bay on its way to landing, the pilot announced that if we would look to our left and down toward the water, we would see a waterspout. My mother had told me stories about the waterspouts she had seen at the Gulf when she was a girl, and I had in my mind the picture she had drawn, of a giant dipper that came down out of the clouds and scooped up the ocean and carried it back up into the sky. Now I craned toward the window from my aisle seat to discover, not a giant dipper at all, but a dark, thin, tornado-like spiral that spun over the surface of the Bay. As I watched, I sensed pressure at my elbow, and I looked to see what it was. All the seats on the right side of the plane had been vacated. The passengers were squeezing into the aisle, stretching forward to look out our windows at the waterspout.

Not long ago, I was standing in a line at a gas station

in Savannah one Saturday afternoon, waiting to pay for my gas, when in the line of people buying and cashing in lottery tickets—the line parallel to mine—a small silver-haired man looked at me and grinned. "I just won five hundred dollars on this ticket!" he said.

Before I could respond, the man behind me said, with evident surprise, "Red?"

There was a pause while the old man with the ticket stared at the one who had spoken. "Paul?"

"Red Spicer? Is that you?" said the man behind me.

"Paul Henderson?"

"Well, I'll be. It *is* you. Red Spicer. I never thought I'd see you again."

The man with the lottery ticket shook his head, grinning. "After all these years."

"Red Spicer. I can't hardly believe it."

The men stepped out of the lines and embraced, patting each other on the back. "You know, I always figured we'd run into each other again one day," said Red.

"You doin' all right, Red?" said Paul. "How's Lucille?"

"Well, Lucy died," said Red. "Been six years in December. Stomach cancer."

"I'm real sorry to hear that," said Paul, shaking his head.

"Yep."

"I dated Lucille. You remember? That was back in 'forty-five. After the war."

"Sure, I remember. Was you introduced us," said Red. "I always did want to thank you for that."

I was watching this exchange carefully, taking fast

notes in a notebook I kept with me, but then it occurred to me that the store had gone quiet. I looked around. Activity had stopped. A middle-aged man at the Coke machine had left his empty cup under the ice dispenser and stepped forward to listen better. The young blonde woman in front of me, the man in glasses behind the counter, the others in the lines, all of us, had turned toward the two men.

The men kept talking, never noticing, I believe, the interest they had excited in the rest of us. Paul had lost a brother. Red had spent a year in counseling at the veterans hospital. Paul had never married. Red's daughter was an architect in California. And there was more.

But gradually, though their conversation continued, the noise of normalcy began to return. I heard a bell ring as the door swung open, heard ice dropping into a paper cup. Someone down the line sneezed, and the man in glasses behind the counter tore a lottery ticket off a roll. My line moved forward a step. Red and Paul returned to their places, vowing to stay in touch.

$\mathcal{I}$ saw a dolphin in the Gulf of Mexico, shaped by the contours of my individual experience. As I move through the paces of my own life, I am separate from others: I build my own world. This is my original relation to the universe, as Emerson wrote.

But to possess a unique and independent reality does not negate the collective character of my human experience. For there is That in an old doctor's wisdom that recollects a wagon train I once saw on a Willacoochee backroad, and there is That in a Tampa Bay waterspout that draws

all the people to the window of a plane, and there is
That in the voices of two old friends who have found each
other again at a gas station in Savannah. It is a sound that
sounds beneath the illusions that keep us separate, and it
binds, and holds, and surprises a crowd of strangers into
quietness.

the solitary life

The eye sinks inward, and the heart lies plain.

MATTHEW ARNOLD

*N*ow this cabin with green window frames and three steps that lead down to the yard is tucked inside eighty acres of tall pines at the end of a long dirt track in the southeastern corner of a rural county where nobody goes who doesn't have business there. It's too far from civilization.

But it does have the modern conveniences. As I said, it has the indoor bathroom. And I put in a phone. But I don't have any hot water and sometimes when it's humid the place smells like mice. I've driven over a copperhead and shot at a cottonmouth and scared off a rattlesnake the size of my right arm. I've watched my neighbor Gene chop the head off a rabid coon and had to quarantine my dogs because they licked it. Around here the ticks leap out of the trees onto strangers, and something about my bathroom attracts spiders.

Nights, too, can be unnerving for people who bristle at the sound of owls whooing and coyotes calling and unseen things rustling in the grass, or who mind the quarter-mile moonlight walk down the drive through the pines to lock the front gate after the guests have all gone home.

*F*or the first few months I lived at the pond, I had no animals for company but the wild, unfamiliar creatures who moved among the trees at night. It was the end of October and I would lie in bed for hours, rigid as a fence post, my senses alive with awareness. Every crunch of leaves outside my window, every gust of wind through the trees, every acorn or twig that hit the cabin's tin roof was a rivet driving my body deeper into the bed.

I remember a weird throbbing, enginelike vibration that used to start out in the woods long after nightfall and go on for hours. I could feel it more than I could hear it: it was like a great chorus of bullfrogs singing an octave too low and just beneath my range of hearing.

I was sure it was a UFO. I could just see troops of stringy, translucent, milk-colored beings, with catlike eyes too big for their faces, all marching in single file through the woods to the cabin, where they would surround my bed and insert miniature transmitters into my ears.

Of course my danger was all imaginary, and somewhere in my rational mind I probably knew the sound was farm equipment, maybe a distant generator or a pump. But at that moment my fear was so real that I could no more have gotten out of that bed than swallowed the pond. I didn't dare move, hardly even dared breathe, for fear of being found out. This was the terror soldiers wrote about, I thought. This was that deep, paralyzing terror they had to face down in order to survive.

By morning, having dozed for only a few hours, I was exhausted and angry.

Growing up I lived half a mile from a prison camp. The place has not been used for years now but the old concrete buildings are still standing, their windows barred with iron and the walls of the tiny cells covered with decades-old graffiti. It's an eerie, forlorn place on the road to the cabin, eight miles away beside the rodeo arena.

As a child I often saw those prisoners in their striped pajamas working on the streets around town, under the scrupulous guard of a mean-looking man holding a gun. Sometimes one of the prisoners would escape and the people in town would have to lock their back doors until he was caught.

Locking back doors was a strange concept to us rural southerners, who never locked any of the doors to our houses or our cars, whether we were in them or not. Back doors, in particular, stayed open, so the milkman could set the milk inside on the floor or friends could leave us a note on the kitchen table. Having to lock *our* back door and put a metal bin in the carport for the milkman darkened my trustful perception of the world and drove the fear of escaped convicts into me for life.

So escaped convicts were another kind of alien I was

thinking about thirty years later as I lay glued to the bed in the cabin, barely breathing, watching the shadows flit by the windows, waiting for daylight. But I was determined to stay put—I'd wanted to live at the pond all my life—so I tried different ways of overcoming my fright. When night came I took the flashlight and practiced walking down to the front gate and back, holding my head up high and whistling that not-afraid song from *The King and I*. I ran up my telephone bill talking to all the friends I'd left behind in Kansas. By the bed I tacked up the Bene Gesserit litany against fear from Frank Herbert's *Dune* novels and repeated it to myself in deep, serious tones before I folded down the covers:

> *I must not fear. Fear is the mind-killer. Fear is the little-death that brings total obliteration. I will face my fear. I will permit it to pass over me and through me. And when it has gone past I will turn the inner eye to see its path. Where the fear has gone there will be nothing. Only I will remain.*

But nothing worked. I was still irrational when the time came to turn out the lamp, which I was afraid to leave on in case some escaped axe murderer who might not otherwise know the cabin existed would see the light by my bed shining through the woods and decide to use the place for a hideout.

Two months later, in December, I went back to Kansas for a long visit and to pick up my cat, Sport, whom I'd left with a friend while I settled in down south. From the day I left the pond to head westward until the day I returned, I never gave my night fears a passing thought, never even talked about them. They had no significance away from the cabin.

I came back to Georgia in late January. That first evening when bedtime arrived, I dutifully recited my litany and waited for the panic to set in. Strangely, it never did.

Since then I've never spent another night sleepless from that kind of fear. Even when escaped convicts really did turn up at my front gate last year at two o'clock in the morning, I didn't get rattled. Anyway they never made it this far down the drive; I expect the sound of Max and Queenie coming at them in the dark scared them off. But I could see their footprints in the soft dirt near the road and they stole the three-wheeler from Gene's barn and hid out in the woods for two days before the sheriff's dogs finally tracked them down.

*E*ven though escaped convicts have found these woods from time to time, visitors are scarce at the pond. In fact, except for the aliens my fancy dreams up, I don't get much company. People don't come and go on their way here and there or call up from town and ask to come out and get to know a little about rustic living, and nobody drops by on a Sunday afternoon for a chat and a glass of sweet tea.

Even my family stays away. They'd rather be where the hot water comes straight from the tap. Or at least where the tap water doesn't give you gas.

Nevertheless, friends, true friends, do come by from time to time. They're the ones who don't mind the spider-webs in the corners of my bathroom or sleeping on the floor. Who don't mind taking a shower with a ladle and a gallon of steaming water from a tin pot, or that the space heater doesn't quite do the job when winter comes. Who don't mind swimming in the pond with the turtles, or flicking the lizards off the screen door before they come inside, or taking long afternoon walks with me in the woods because that's the only entertainment I've got to offer.

They come because of me, after all. They come because they're more interested in me than the things I've put around me. They're not hung up on where I live, or what I'm wearing, or what I've got. They don't come around often—not out to this old cabin, not even in a lifetime. And I don't always recognize them at first.

I don't have many friends like that, and the ones I do have are scattered all over the country. But when they do find the time to bring themselves so far past the world of comforts and conveniences and come out to the pond, their visits always invest my life with a richness I had never known before. For days after someone is gone, I can still trace our footprints where we walked the edges of fields looking for arrowheads, still see where the dirt gathered around the edges of our shoes. I can see where we leaned down to examine the deer moss under the twisted pine on the old logging trail, or where we stopped to marvel over wild magnolias all in bloom and the horsehair ferns that cluster under cypresses and black gums by the swamp. Maybe the paddles are still wet from when we took the boat out on the water, searching for beaver sign or bream beds. In the fall, I might find the hulls from the peanuts we ate raw off the vines or the flattened grass where we found tufts of coyote fur. In summer, I might find empty wineglasses by the sofa where we sat talking late into the evening, gathered in by the closeness of the night air and the songs of bullfrogs and crickets and whippoorwills that ring around the pond.

Times like these hold a kind of truth all their own. It's in the simplicity of their character, in the clarity of intention between the two of us, where for a while what we're thinking, what we're saying, and what we're feeling all come together and we let our words out loose and unclut-tered, and our movements are honest and unstudied. For a while all the various sides of my nature—the part of me that's tough, the part of me that's vulnerable, the part of me that's kind—they blend together into a kind of graceful whole, like grasses woven into basket, pictures resolving into story. And then suddenly there I am, shoving the boat out onto the pond my complete and utter self, in perfect harmony with another complete and utter self who is reaching out a hand to help me in. In those moments, I find out who I am.

Solitude is an easy companion. It doesn't require much from me except the ability to be comfortable alone. Friends need more. They need my attention, my energy, and my time. On the whole, I prefer solitude. Even so, I wouldn't trade the times I've spent at the pond with my friends for twice the solitary hours those times have cost me. For real friends are generous: they leave behind the warmth of their company for my memory to wrap itself around, along with the remarkable gift of having taught me to know my self.

And solitude, too, teaches. I have no idea why I no longer have to lie in bed like a clenched fist. Somehow between the coming home and the going away and the coming back again, my night fears passed through me and, like the litany says, I was all that remained. Perhaps it was only a habit I had gotten into, broken with my leaving. Now I walk around outside at night often, because I'm fond of the way moonlight leaves shadows on the trails and silver on the water. On cloudless nights, the Milky Way is a lightened path through an obsidian sky.

It's after midnight in late February now, and I've been sitting on the back steps, bathed in air warm enough for bare feet and a T-shirt, crowded in by the dogs. Comforts are immanent here on these mild star-filled nights, although it took me a while to find them. There's something soothing in the way the trees breathe the rhythm of the wind ebbing and flowing through the leaves, like the sea heard from an open window, and waves moving in and out on the sand, moving in and out. It's a rhythm of calm. A rhythm of quiet, of sleep and easy dreaming. A night rhythm, free of intellect and unencumbered. I breathe, and the air holds no scent but one of darkness clean and clear. The sky is deep blue-black, cloudless, the red crescent of moon, gone. I can see Orion above me, in the open space ringed by the upper branches of the pines that hug the water. A thousand frog voices, chattering and squeaking and chirping or with notes drawn out deep and long, echo around the pond. Theirs is another rhythm, a separate rhythm, from the rhythm of the trees. Inside, the cabin air is warm and close, with a hint of the cedar I burned this morning.

I confess that in the dark I am still afraid of storms. Old trees have a way of falling in high winds, and one diseased pine at the edge of the pond has lost a chunk out of its middle and only needs a sudden southerly gust to twist it down onto this tarpaper shack. Lightning, also, favors those trees. But I remind myself that this place has survived all the storms of my lifetime; it will last, I suppose, until summer, when like Huck Finn I'll have to light out for the territory, on the next stage of my journey.

minding the fort

When I found my dog Max three years ago, I was on my weekend trip to Wal-Mart in a neighboring town twenty miles from my cabin and he was sitting on the bare edge of a gravel road, scratching, his pink puppy tummy stuck out as round and tight as a water balloon. It was a sunny early-March morning, cool and blue and full up with the coming of spring, and I was in the mood for a dog, so I picked him up. Max and I bonded instantly, he having done me the courtesy of decorating the floor of my truck with an infinite number of tapeworms and driving my vet bill up to a respectably middle-class number from which—since the addition of

Queenie and a succession of stray cats—my great potential has yet to redeem me.

The vet gave Max shots for every conceivable internal parasite and pills for those parasites the shots wouldn't kill and a bottle of insecticide with a skull and crossbones on the label for the mange mites that were literally eating Max alive from the outside in. Max spent the next eight weeks in a long cedar box I dragged from the bed to the computer in the morning and from the computer back to the bed at night. He suffered through weekly baths in poison one drop of which turned three gallons of water into something that looked like skim milk but smelled like a bacteriological accident. All day long when he wasn't sleeping he scratched, crying in frustration as the mites burrowed deeper and deeper into his tortured skin.

But he survived and the mites didn't and gradually his hair grew back over those bare pink patches. Now he has lots of hair, a wiry blend of black and white with some brown on his face for variety. His feet are too big for his frame and so are his ears, which stand straight out from his head like wings, except that one sometimes flops forward like a flag on a still day. When he sits in the long grass, all I can see are his ears. His back legs are as bowed as a Wyoming cowboy's. He trots everywhere he goes, holding his foot-long tail bolt upright, which makes him prissy. But he's all muscle. Gene says, "He's a hard little dog, ain't he." He has brown eyes and an attentive expression and I can't tell whether he's smart or just sneaky.

Nobody really knows what kind of dog Max is, but people like to guess. One of my neighbors says Max is a blue heeler. Another says he's a dingo. Gene says he's a feist. A friend of mine says he looks like Yoda, but of course Yoda's no dog. Personally, I think Max is the result of a late-night tryst between a German shepherd and a female Chihuahua before the Chihuahua ran off with a pit bull. I realize that this theory has no ground in ordinary genetics—but then I think, neither does Max.

Whatever Max is made up of, my constant nursing of him during his early life never spoiled him into the fluffy, treat-craving, mild-mannered lap dog that my German shepherd Queenie has turned out to be. Queenie prefers air-conditioning and if I ever let her indoors where it's cool, I have to blackmail her with Milk-Bones to get her back out again. When Max goes roaming around the neighborhood, Queenie lies by the gate all day long and barks at noises and if something startles her she smashes herself against my legs for protection. She didn't shed tapeworms all over my new car the day I brought her home from the breeder, but the severe case of hookworm that I didn't know she had did not leave the scent of roses in the back seat, nor in Donnie's crop-duster hangar up the hill where I left her for five minutes nor on any of his airplane magazines that his wife was sorting on the floor.

So Queenie is a lush. Max, however, is a dog's dog; he's essence of dog. The day I let him out of his cedar box for good, he rolled in a dead thing and paraded around the yard reeking for days. Although he's only a third her size I've seen him terrorize Queenie to distraction, attack the bulldog down the road, run Gene's bull, bite the kicking end of an armadillo, and face up to a cottonmouth that looked big enough to swallow his head. He once barked some animal all the way around the pond at three o'clock in the morning. I've watched him run deer through the woods and break an otter's neck with one lightning jerk. The fence doesn't exist that can hold him in. He has scratched at the concrete blocks that stopped him from squeezing under the gate until they've crumbled into dust. He's the unbounded spirit of independence. He's unbounded spirit. He has to run and I have to let him.

Still, as independent and unfettered as Max likes to be, and as mindless as Queenie seems, the dogs have these rituals that they measure out their lives by. When I get in the car to drive to town, Max stands beside the car until he finds out whether I'm going to take him with me. If he gets to go, he climbs carefully into the back seat behind me— first one paw up, then the others. He refuses to sit in the front. If I move him to the front, he turns around and goes to the back again. He doesn't seem to mind where we're going, he just wants to go. Sometimes he looks out the window, but mostly he sleeps.

Queenie, on the other hand, won't go voluntarily into the car at all. If she knows she's got to go in the car, all her ninety pounds go limp and I have to pick her up and pour her in, which is no small feat, considering that I almost don't outweigh her.

When Max was little he used to chase the car down the highway. I hated that; it made me cringe, him tearing down the middle of the paved road after me with a Mack truck bearing down on him from behind. But he got tired of all that hard work running and no reward, I guess, and now he just follows me to the front gate and watches until I'm out of sight. Then he trots across the road and spends the rest of the day at Gene's. "Max comes a-running up here soon's you leave," Gene says. "I don't believe he likes it down at your place."

If the temperature drops below freezing and I let the

dogs in for the night, at daybreak Queenie climbs into the bed with me and lies down at full length with her head on the pillow and her back against mine. She knows better than to get on the furniture, but I can't get her off that bed in the morning no matter how hard I try. If I shove her, she just grunts and shoves back. If I get up and try to pull her off the bed, she hangs on to the comforter so hard she digs holes in it, but by that time I'm laughing so hard it doesn't matter anyway.

Sometimes Max stands at the edge of the pond and barks at the water for hours. I don't know what he sees. Light, maybe. Minnows. Dragonflies. At night, he walks around the yard picking his feet up like a heron. I think he dislikes being spooked by frogs and crickets and lizards that move around suddenly in the grass.

But there's another side to the dogs that isn't so easy to know. Max kills, often and indiscriminately, and it's an instinct he's brought out in Queenie. Together they've made a serious dent in the armadillo population, but I can stand that; and I've gotten used to finding the ravaged squirrels and rats and raccoons, snakes, and occasional birds laid out in state in the yard. The baby possums and Alice's runaway kitten were harder to take.

As time has passed, this tendency in the dogs has intensified. I was running down a dirt road one afternoon last summer when a beagle Max had befriended came barking out from some bushes and ran up to meet us. Max went for his throat. Queenie was right behind him. I managed to pull the dogs apart and the beagle got away, but I began to see that around small live things now the dogs would go feral. It occurred to me that I wouldn't want them to play with children. So maybe I shouldn't have been surprised the day I found my long-haired calico cat, Grace, dead on the bank of the pond.

Grace was the ultimate pet cat, the one who overturned all the stereotypes people don't like about cats. She was never aloof: she liked to sit in strangers' laps and fold herself into the hollows my body made in the bed at night. She never ignored me if paying attention didn't suit her mood: like a puppy, she always came galloping across the room when I called her. She didn't spew hair balls or throw up under chairs, and she didn't shovel litter out of the cat box or leave little spiteful presents on the bedspread. As far as I could tell, I never got on her nerves. Wherever I sat, she sat, too.

Grace was, however, insistent about trying to get outside. She was a stray when somebody gave her to me, so maybe, like Max, she still had the highway in her blood. When I left the door open, she'd stand at the screen for hours, gazing out. If I went outside, she'd try to slip out before the screen slammed shut. Many times she made it and I had to catch her and bring her back in. Now, this made me feel something like a prison warden, because it was clear that Grace really wanted to be an outside cat. But I'd had her declawed because she was tearing up the rattan, and I had to make her stay in. I figured that claws wouldn't have given her a fighting chance against the German shepherd and that wild-eared Max anyway.

But on this particular night Grace had gotten out without my knowing, which had never happened before. I'd been busy, cleaning out closets, going in and out of the cabin. I'd caught her outside once already and thought of putting her in the bathroom until I was through, but I didn't.

Two days later I was coming back across the dam, looking for her, when from a distance I saw her long body stretched out by the water. The pure white fur on her neck was still clean and soft; the rest of her was covered in mud. Her yellow eyes were open. The dogs looked at me indifferently as I picked her up by the throat and carried her into the yard.

A few days earlier I had run right past a steel trap in the woods and Max, running behind me, stuck his paw into it. It took an eternity of listening to him howl before I could figure out how to get him free. I remembered wondering at the time whether I'd better be on the alert, because that's the way things go in my life. I get a signal, and then something happens. Sometimes I'm prepared: it depends on whether I'm attending.

The instant of my inattention was the point of greatest peril. With Grace, the signs were there for me to read, but in my preoccupation I didn't see them. Her death caught me in an act of naked carelessness and of course I've put myself through all the self-flagellation routines. I berate myself that those cries I now remember hearing in my sleep the night she died did not awaken me. I wasn't attending. How could I not have noticed she was gone? Maybe those claws could have saved her; what was I thinking, that I would wipe out her defenses in order to save a stick of furniture?

Part of me does not deny my innocence in the affair: my forgetfulness was not deliberate, nor was my affection for Grace insincere. Certainly the dogs are not to blame.

Still, there is no balm for the open wound of lost companionship, where death has stolen into your fortress and rent the whole cloth of your complacency to shreds. In your chagrin, in your shame, in your justification against the accusation of neglect, in your defiance against the challenge of your thoughtless choices there is only wielding a hoe, splitting the roots of a maple tree, gouging out a hole in the hard earth to bury the cat in. And the medieval poets understood the futility of the gesture. In the end, they said, it doesn't pay to forget that the only territorial authority is death, and it can catch you by surprise.

Ne noghte es sekire to youreselfe in certayne bot dethe,
And he es so uncertayne that sodaynly he comes.

snakes on the path

"Watch out for snakes, dearie."

MaRe

$\mathcal{S}$nakes are ubiquitous but I try not to think about it.

When I moved to the pond, MaRe told me that water moccasins could get into the toilet bowl through the plumbing so I should never sit down without looking. She told me that water moccasins would crawl into the boat with me when I went fishing and that rattlesnakes would come in through the windows if I left them open. I shouldn't walk around outside in the dark, she said, because poisonous snakes moved around at night. She told me that rattlesnakes would curl up on the driveway and if I wasn't careful they'd bite me when I opened the gate. They lived under the house, she said. She told me that if a cotton-mouth ever saw me it would chase me as far as I could run and that I should never, ever go swimming in the pond.

I moved to the cabin in October and it was early summer before I saw my first snake. By then, I had become less cautious about looking for them and when this one raised its head and I saw that it wasn't a big orange stick I was about to step on, it nearly scared me senseless. The thing was huge—three feet long at least and as big around as my wrist. It was lying beside the cabin next to the water hose, which I was bending down to pick up so I could water the tomatoes.

I froze. I was sure the thing was poisonous. It was probably a cottonmouth. Look how triangular the head was. An orange cottonmouth. I knew I should have gotten that snake book. I need to kill it, I thought.

But what if I was wrong and it just ate mice?

Better not take chances, I thought. When in doubt, kill it.

I backed away. I was going for the gun, an old six-shooter my friend Mr. Norman had lent me for emergencies.

Okay, I thought. If it chases me when I run, I'll know it's a cottonmouth.

I reached the screen door and looked behind me. No snake.

Okay then, I thought. If it's still there when I get back with the gun, I'll say it's poisonous.

I ran in and grabbed the pistol and a handful of bullets and ran back out. The snake hadn't moved.

I knew it, I thought. Poisonous.

I shot all six bullets at that snake—twice, which

means I reloaded—and never hit it once. All that time, it just watched me. On the thirteenth try I hit it near the middle. I didn't kill it, but I could tell that it was hurt. It writhed some, but it stayed put.

In frustration, I went back inside and called Gene, and he sent his grandson over with a nine-millimeter pistol. Well, that ought to do it, I thought.

But Brian couldn't hit the snake either, until the sixth shot, while it was trying to crawl away. The snake opened its mouth and raised itself off the ground and swayed back and forth, back and forth, in a wide arc.

"If snakes can scream, this one is screaming," I said. The sight was awful to watch and it made me want to take everything back. But of course it was way too late for that.

Then Gene showed up with his shotgun and blasted the snake in the head. We looked for fangs and for pits behind the snake's eyes, but we couldn't find them.

Altogether I'd say that snake had died for the better part of an hour. Gene threw it in the creek, and we all smelled it for a long time. Max was pretty pleased about that.

A few weeks later Mr. Norman told me I'd killed a corn snake. They're not poisonous, he said. They just eat mice—along with rats, birds, and bats. They're one of the most beautiful snakes in North America, he said. In captivity, they can live almost twenty-two years.

One day the dogs wouldn't stop barking, so I went outside to see why. They were standing near the back steps, staring up at some trees near the pond. I couldn't imagine what in the trees could get them so excited, so I walked over to a live oak by the water and then I saw them—twenty feet up, two big copperheads, hanging from a branch. I recognized them instantly: I can't say why. They were twining around each other at full length, mating. The ritual was stunning to watch. Primeval. A terrible beauty, as Yeats wrote.

But these copperheads were not like the corn snake: they could kill the dogs. I needed to get rid of them. This time, instead of wasting shot, I went right in and called Gene. He came over in the truck with Alice, and maybe the disturbance alerted the snakes, because they dropped down out of the tree as soon as Gene drove into the yard. Still, he was able to kill one copperhead on the ground. The other one got away, but the next day the dogs found it by the fence and I ran over it with the car.

Copperhead bites are painful, I learned later, but they rarely pose a serious threat to life.

I did find a snake in the bathroom once but it wasn't in the toilet.

I had brought MaRe out to the cabin so I could brag on all the preparations I'd made for moving in. She was as tenacious as ever but weak and unsteady, and she couldn't walk very fast with her hand-painted cane. She was standing in the bathroom door, and I was about to show off my pink flamingo shower curtain when I noticed a faint dead-animal smell coming from under the sink. So I opened the cabinet door and found myself staring into the black beady eyes of a pine snake, which at the time I took to be the fabled toilet bowl moccasin.

"Snake!" I yelled, and nearly knocked MaRe down as I raced by her on my way to the other end of the cabin.

"Where?" she cried. She, of course, was not as speedy as I, and when I turned around to answer her she was just shuffling out of the doorway. I went back to help her, but the snake had disappeared down the hole around the drainpipe.

I found another pine snake on the steps one morning but by then I was pretty smart about snakes, having bought a book and learned what to look for. I picked that snake up on the end of my walking stick and flipped it over the fence.

One day I drove into the yard and found Max standing in the space where I usually park, barking frantically at a fat coiled cottonmouth. I knew it was a cottonmouth because its dark gray head was in the air and its open white mouth was the size of my palm.

I grabbed Max up in my arms—I didn't have Queenie yet—and I raced in to get Mr. Norman's gun . . . checking my heels to see if I was being chased. I wasn't.

I left Max in the cabin and ran back outside. My hands were shaking. The cottonmouth was still there, still coiled, still gaping. I fired six shots and missed. I ran back inside to reload, but in my panic I'd forgotten how. By the time I remembered, the cottonmouth was gone.

There was one other snake I tried to kill—a timber rattler the dogs found wrapped around some fallen logs by the back gate. After three misses with Mr. Norman's gun, I gave up and let him go and now I don't shoot at snakes any more.

Snakes are ubiquitous, and they come in all colors and sizes. Some of them just eat the mice, and some of them can kill you. Some can get right up next to you on the path before you even know they're there. I still remember MaRe's warnings, and I don't go swimming in the pond, but Queenie does. I've never had a water moccasin try to climb into the boat with me and I've never seen one in the toilet. There are rattlesnake nests under the cabin, but I've never known a rattlesnake to come through an open window, and except for that timber rattler the dogs found by the gate I've never seen one on the driveway. I've never seen a cottonmouth chase anything.

Two months ago, I saw my last snake of the season while I was coming back from a walk. It was a young water moccasin, curled up beneath some blackberry vines on the dam, right in the middle of the trail. I almost didn't see him in time, he was so still, and the dogs missed him altogether. I stopped and looked at him a minute. Then I went on to the cabin and made some sweet tea.

keeper of the tribe

There is a bend in the eastward path at the far end of the Dills' cotton field where I often stand and watch the wind in the pines that edge the rows upon rows of cotton. In the fall, after the farmers bale the cotton and turn the deep earth up to await the spring planting, I watch for a hard rain to wash the dirt off the rocks and then a long spell of bright days for the fields to dry and lighten in the sun. That's when I go hunting for the fluted arrowheads, the stone knives, the shards of pottery that speak of the lives of those others who minded this land when it was still forest and creek, before it was shaped into field and pond. I like to turn the evidence of those others over in my hands, examine the patterns of slender rope pressed into the clay pot rims, marvel at the sharpness and symmetry of the points, wondering which were the ones for birds, which for deer, which for fish.

When I hold these things, I can envision the ones who made them. I can look up from the piece of clay in my palm toward the edge of the wood and see the encampment there, at the far end of the field, in a clearing just up the slope from the creek. Not far from a live oak, a woman squats beside her small fire, scooping a hole in the embers. Her daughter kneels beside her, taking meal from a bowl and patting it into thin cakes in her hands. By a separate fire, another woman blows embers into flame, then calls to a boy whose grandfather is teaching him to knap flint. Two girls work at opposite ends of a deer hide, scraping away the flesh, and its pungence comes to me on the breeze. At the edge of the camp, a short man stands straight and quiet, looking on. He wears leggings, but his chest and feet are bare. His right hand holds a spear, its tip pointing skyward.

To my right, the path through the field winds away southward, then disappears down a low hill and into the woods, where it widens into an old logging road. The road crosses the dam at the alligator pond, then wanders past the twisted pine and onward another mile to the swamp. After a long stretch of rainless days, you can follow that road all the way through the swamp to a small, high clearing that is almost perfectly round.

Ringed by water oaks, cypress trees, black gums, and a sprawling primitive undergrowth of mosses, palmettos, ferns, and pale pink swamp honeysuckle, the earth there is covered in clover and deep-colored ground ivies that bloom only in that damp, fragrant darkness. Mosquitoes and water bugs and dragonflies with iridescent blue wings thrive around the tea-colored water of the Willacoochee River branch that twines around the cypresses and overflows its low banks to make the clearing inaccessible in wet weather, except by boat.

The road ends in that clearing now. But ten mossy pilings still stand high out of the water where a railroad trestle once led into the clearing from the long stretch of forest on the far side of the branch. In the trunks of the trees that border the lower-lying places, rusted spikes show where the train carried its load of pines back to the pulp mills closer to town.

I gave my sister a tour of the swamp on a late July afternoon in sweltering heat. Stupidly carrying no water, and having bathed in bug spray that did little to daunt the stinging yellowflies, now we were picking our way over the exposed tree roots and around the wide puddles of black silt that covered the swamp floor, keeping watch for moccasins and the alligators I'd never seen back there but was positive were only hiding in the shadows, masquerading as logs.

I was thirsty and a little spooked, but I was playing the big-sister part well enough, forging fearlessly ahead of Kelly to reach the edge of that first stretch of swamp, batting away the low-hanging Spanish mosses, poking my walking stick into the thick grasses that covered the path to the clearing. Kelly was miserable. The bandanna I had tied around my head was keeping the insecticide-laden sweat out of my eyes, but Kelly's baseball cap wasn't doing the same for her, and her eyes were puffy and red. Still, she didn't want to turn back, and we were about to cross one of the low spots near the clearing when I stopped.

"Don't move," I said, turning quickly to look back at Kel.

She stopped. "What? What is it?"

"Snake," I said. "Big one. By that tree." I nodded toward a cypress tree a yard away on my left.

Her shoulders stiffened. "Oh God," she said.

"Where're the dogs?"

"I don't know. Somewhere behind us."

"Good. Keep still."

I craned my neck so I could see better. The snake was blueblack and shiny, as long and as thick as the cypress knee it lay wrapped around. "I think it ate something," I said. "There's a hump in the middle."

Kelly looked. "Is that a moccasin?"

"Just a minute," I said. The snake was lethargic and didn't seem to notice us. I took a tentative step toward it, trying to get a closer look at its head. Not flat. Good. No pits behind the eyes. Good. Way too big to be a cotton-mouth, I thought.

"Indigo snake," I pronounced. I took a breath. "They're harmless." I pointed my walking stick at it, and it slithered away into the swamp just as the dogs came running around the corner.

"Indigo snake?" Kelly said. "I've never heard of that."

"Well, that's not the only thing that's back here," I said, "so keep your eyes open."

We walked on.

Kelly had never seen the swamp, and I'd been there

only a few times myself: too much rain. I was curious to see how she would respond to it. There were some tree-covered bluffs in eastern Kansas that I almost owned once. I called the place Many Paths. The first time I saw it, I burst into tears. So did Kelly.

The clearing is like that. There is something about it that touches you, that makes you feel raw and open—a kind of sincerity. At Many Paths, it was the quiet, I think, or the rustling of all those hardwoods or, after a rain, the creek moving over rocks. Down in the swamp, it is the echoes of men's voices, the crack and rush of trees falling on trees, the keening of a train whistle that no longer sounds, yet sounds still in the scarred trunks of the cypresses, the rusted spikes, the vanished trestle, the road.

When we got to the clearing, I pointed out the pilings, and Kelly went down by the water to look at them. The dogs plopped down on the bank beside her. I went looking for owl feathers and left her to herself.

It is the night before, and it is late. Kelly and I are sitting on the sofa in the cabin, drinking wine. The only light is from my last candle, which has now burned down to a stub. The cabin door is open, but there is no breeze, and the night air is balmy and close.

I am telling Kelly about the swamp, how I hope we can get through to the clearing the next day, how I'm hoping it won't rain. "Don't let me forget the bug spray," I say. "Did you bring your running shoes?"

"Uh-huh," she says. She is making shadow puppets on the ceiling. In the candlelight, the forms flicker in and out of the darkness. She makes a swan.

"Good one, Kel," I tell her. "All I can do is a rabbit." I make a rabbit. That is, I stick up two fingers and wiggle them.

"What's this?" Kelly says, crooking her wrist to form a witch with a bent nose.

"Amazing," I say. "How'd you do that?"

She shows me but I can't make the nose bend. It is her hands. I am always surprised by my sister's hands. She is thirty-two now, but her hands still seem the same to me as when she was twelve. They are delicate, finely shaped, sensitive hands, and they have made her an exceptional pianist and a far more artful guitarist than I.

"My fingers won't do right," I grumble.

"You can do this one," she says, and she straightens her hands and makes two straight lines separated by a width of white space.

"What's that?"

"Me and Sean," she says. Sean is Kelly's husband. After eight years, they are breaking up.

"Oh," I say. There is nothing else. In a dozen long-distance phone calls, we've already said it all.

I make Kelly a place to sleep out of blankets and Therm-a-Rest pads on the floor next to my bed, and we settle down. She asks me to leave the candle, but it soon burns out.

I am lying on my back with my arms folded under my head, waiting for sleep but not really sleepy, listening to the frogs and the cicadas, excited about showing Kelly the clearing in the swamp. Eventually, after a long while, a sound creeps into my awareness, and it dawns on me that she is crying, that she has been crying for some time, that she is trying to muffle the sound with her pillow.

"Kelly?" I whisper. "Kel?"

She doesn't answer. I listen and fidget, feeling awkward and inadequate.

Then suddenly she isn't crying any more. She has shoved the pillow aside and she is *weeping*, and it is that bottom-of-the-soul weeping, that all-out despairing weeping that begins soft and slow and a little sad but before long winds itself out into something that feels like the fresh reopening of every wound that ever left a scar.

I hate this. I have always hated it when Kelly cries, but this is way beyond crying. This is not something simple, something that will wear itself down after a few minutes of my silent discomfort, and I am lost inside the sound of it, having not the least idea how to handle it.

Or rather, knowing exactly how to handle it, but unable to do it. I am not one to curl up in the blankets with my little sister and fold my arms around her, like all those wonderful Victorians in the novels, like when Jane Eyre climbs into the bed with her frail best friend Helen Burns and holds her while she dies. My family isn't given to that kind of intimacy. Oh, I love Kelly enough to do it, God knows, and I long to do it, would give anything to cradle her like that, rock her, stroke her hair, say soothing things to her until her weeping subsides. But I just cannot do it.

There is something else, too, that is keeping my stomach clenched and my arms stiff at my sides, something I have only begun to understand since the drama of Kelly's divorce has woven itself into the patterns of my own life.

From the time my parents separated when I was seventeen, I've felt the mantle of family caretaker settle on my shoulders as the older sister. I need to be the strong one, undaunted, unshakable: I have to mind the womenfolk, take care of the ones who have been left in my protection. So when they suffer, their suffering falls hard on me. Because if I suffer too much with them I might let my guard down. I might even disappear. It is who I am: that strong one.

I know what it is for Kelly, this divorce. I went through it over and over and then over again myself between the ages of nineteen and twenty-nine, although never with a marriage as solid as hers has seemed. But it was hell anyway. Always, always, always. My mother endured it, and then I, and now Kelly, and I know what it is, and everything it is, and everything it feels like. But all I can offer is words.

"I hate to see you like this," I say finally into the dark, when I can stand my reticence no longer.

"I know," she manages to say between sobs.

"It's because I can't fix it, Kel," I say. "I want to fix it, but I can't."

"I know. I'll be okay. I just need some . . . time."

"I love you," I blurt. "But it's not enough. It doesn't feel like enough."

There is a silence.

"Kelly?" I say.

"It's enough," she says. And again, more softly: "It's enough."

I picked an ivy blossom and took it to Kelly where she was sitting under a cypress tree beside the river. The dogs had left her side and were wandering around farther back in the swamp, where the water had receded. Kelly was rubbing her eyes, and I must have had one of those big-sister looks on my face because she said quickly, before I could ask, "I'm okay, Ame," and she smiled and pushed her baseball cap back on her head.

"Your eyes are really red," I said.

"Well, at least I cried all the bug spray out." She looked away, toward the pilings. "It's this place."

"I know," I said. "That's why I wanted you to see it."

"It's like Many Paths," she said. "It gets to you."

"Yeah. That's what I thought, too."

I stood a minute, watching the water. "Well," I said, "you ready? I have some more stuff to show you."

"Okay," she said.

I called the dogs and we left.

So on our hike back to the field, I pointed out the deer skull with the teeth still in it that Mom and I had found on a hike to the swamp four years ago, and the cow graveyard, and the twisted pine with the moss on the north side, and the spot where Max got caught in the steel trap and cried and cried and I felt terrible because it took me so long to get him out, and the piece of garden hose left behind by rattlesnake hunters after they gassed a gopher turtle den, and the rusted beaver trap with the door that wouldn't close, and I was about to show her where an otter had humped up some pine straw at the alligator pond when she stopped. "Ame?" she said.

"Huh," I said. I was busy examining the pine straw. "Hey, look at this. Fish-scale otter scat."

"Ame?"

The tone in her voice made me look up. "What is it?"

"How did you know it was an indigo snake?"

"Oh," I said. "Practice. They're everywhere."

"They are?"

"Ubiquitous."

"Oh."

"They come in through the windows," I said. "Get into the toilet. Lie around on the steps. You have to get to know them. Look at this." I pointed to the scat.

"I see," she said. "It's pink."

"Been eating crawdads," I said.

"Crawdads are pink?"

"Yeah."

"Oh."

When we got back to the Dills' cotton field, I took Kelly to the spot where I liked to stand.

"Look out there, Kel," I said, pointing to the live oak at the far end of the field. "That's where they were. It's like I can see them." I told her about the campground, and the women at their fires, and the man looking on from the edge of the encampment, holding the spear. "It's why I look for arrowheads," I said, which was an interest Kelly didn't share and had wondered at in me.

"But now it makes sense," she said. "That's you."

"What's me?"

"*He's* you," she said. "I mean, just look at you."

"What?"

She pointed to my walking stick. "That's your spear," she said.

"Oh."

"You're watching, he's watching," she said. "Just look how you're standing."

I looked down at my feet, my wide stance, my walking stick, then looked back at my sister. It is one of the reasons I like her. She sees things I can't see.

We started for the cabin. Kelly stayed on the path while I walked between two rows of cotton, scanning the ground. It didn't take long to find it, even though it was half buried. It was white flint, sharply triangular, with edges so fine it still could have cut through leather.

the condition of not-seeing

$\mathcal{M}$y third ex-husband Terry flew airplanes for a living, so it's not surprising that he should have good eyes. This was particularly helpful during pheasant-hunting season.

Terry could see a pheasant standing in a milo field where the milo was still four feet tall. He could see a pheasant hiding in prairie grass. He could see a pheasant huddling in the underbrush, or marching down a wind-break, or pecking at gravel in the road half a mile ahead. Terry could see a pheasant in an ice storm, a blizzard, and on those overcast winter days right before it snows when all the color washes out of the world and every rock, tree, creek, and bird is the same shade of gray.

Me, I could never see pheasants.

"He's right there. Under that hedge apple tree," Terry would whisper while I reached for the Browning twenty-gauge shotgun he had given me for my birthday.

"*Which* hedge apple tree?" I'd ask, squinting at a row of hedge apple trees thirty feet away.

"Right *there*," he'd say, pointing.

Then the pheasant would fly up out of the underbrush. Then I'd see it.

After I came back down to Georgia and moved to the pond, my friend Richard used to come looking for arrowheads with me in the fields. He came for a year before he moved to Florida, always waiting for the best times—after the plowing and then a good rain and a dry spell. But he never found any arrowheads.

I could always find arrowheads. I could see them. Sometimes if the sun was right I could see them from a long way off. I once saw a white spear point glinting on a mound of dirt twenty paces away. Two years ago, I found half a flint knife at the back of Gene's rye field near the graveyard. Last year, after the summer rains and the planting and harvesting of two crops, I found the other half.

Before I started finding arrowheads, I found feathers. I once found a blue heron feather caught in some blackberry vines on the dam. I found an owl feather in the Harpers' abandoned barn and a bluebird feather on the dirt road by Gene's house and a woodpecker feather in a rotted tree trunk by the creek. Then one day I found an arrowhead. I started looking for arrowheads when I went walking. After that I couldn't find feathers any more.

$\mathcal{O}$ne day I tried to find a feather anyway, just to prove I could still do it. I looked under the pines behind the cabin, where the owls live. I looked in the blackberry vines on the dam and on the trails in the woods and by the alligator pond on the way to the swamp. I looked all afternoon, but I never found a single feather. I did find a broken flint point, though, on my way back through the field. A few days later, my cousin came to visit and found two hawk feathers by the west gate.

I wasn't sure why Terry could always see pheasants and I couldn't find feathers any more. I didn't know why Richard never found arrowheads and I had a bowl full of them by the lamp. But then I thought of what Krishnamurti had said about conditioning, that until I could open my awareness to everything around me, I'd only be able to see what I had always seen. I'd have no peripheral vision. So I was conditioned to see arrowheads, and my attention was blind to feathers.

When I saw how narrow my focus had been, I began to wonder what in my preoccupation with arrowheads I'd been missing besides feathers. I wondered if I went out walking and didn't look for anything, I would see everything.

So I tried it. But it's not easy and I'm not good at it, walking through fields without scanning the ground for flint points. In my concentration, I ignore the weathered tobacco barn across the greening cotton field, the silver-blue surface of the Dills' pond reflecting the spring sky, and in the water the thin, bleached tree stumps that from a distance might be a flotilla of tiny sailing ships with their sails furled about their masts. Strolling down the logging trails, I am caught by the bird down beside a fallen magnolia leaf, the tracks of a raccoon, a wildflower I've never seen—and never notice the scent of mimosa blossoming at the edge of the wood until I have passed it by, until I remember and wrench myself free to feel the heat of the day again, the dampness of my T-shirt against my skin.

But I keep practicing, and sometimes I discover a rare moment of not-seeing, when my awareness is not bound in by the sharp spotlight of the eyes and mind, when my vision opens out into the whole wide range of the experience of the out-of-doors. Not long ago I was standing in Gene's peanut field, just breathing in, the way a person does after a rain, watching a hawk ride a thermal and noticing how the sky shimmers in midsummer. After a while, I began to walk—and at the edge of my boot I discovered a flawless arrowhead, the color of clay. Later, on the way back to the cabin, I knelt down to examine a beaver print and at the edge of my vision I glimpsed an owl feather. It was blowing back and forth in the breeze, held out like a present on the tip of a plum branch beside the pond.

too many shoes and other attachments

In eastern Kansas, out in the country, there's a wide stretch of wood and field where some monks live, and they let guests stay there from time to time. Before I moved back down to Georgia, I used to spend weekends in their hermitages, getting away from the city, where I was tied up with running my business from morning to night.

The first time I went to this place, I took along two gallons of water, several rolls of toilet paper, and a cooler packed with so much food I could have invited the whole community for a party. I also took a backpack full of clothes, hiking boots, tennis shoes, flip-flops, bug spray, sunblock, books, my guitar, and some other stuff. When I got there, one of the monks had to help me carry it all, a half-mile back through the woods to my cabin.

My hermitage, Willow, was a tiny wooden box with a sloping roof on stilts in the deep forest. If I stood in the center of the single room and stretched out both arms, I could just about touch the opposite walls. But there was a window on every wall, which gave the place some sense of space, and a porch out front with a chair where I could stow my cooler, my jugs of water, and all those shoes I thought I'd need.

The bed was a narrow wooden platform nailed to the wall, covered by a hard mattress and a thin pillow. One corner of the cabin held a desk with a straight-backed wooden chair, a prayer book, and some candles in a tin. I spied, with some discomfort, a chamber pot on the floor. Behind the door, which was held open by a rock, I found a broom, a dustpan, and some hooks nailed to the wall. On those hooks I hung up a few of the clothes I'd brought.

My things put away, so far as was possible, I pulled off my hiking boots, put on my flip-flops, sat down at the desk, and went through all the drawers. I tried to think up things to do. The idea of two days stretching out before me and nothing to fill them with—that was a problem. Never mind that I'd come here to slow down: I couldn't stand the thought of being bored.

So I updated the balance in my checkbooks. I sat outside in the chair on the porch until I got cold. I put my boots back on and walked to the stone circle in the field, where I tried to sit still on a rock—until I got cold and had to come back to Willow to put on a sweater.

I marched around the cabin, reinspecting everything

and opening all the windows. I swept the floor. I swept the porch. I put on my tennis shoes and walked to the lodge, where on a shelf I found a book I wanted to read. I took the book outside and sat on the steps, took off my shoes, read some of the book, got bored with it, put my shoes back on. I took a long time getting the laces straight. Then I tied the laces. Then I untied them and tied them again more neatly.

Then I went in and put the book back on the shelf, filled a paper sack with bananas, cheese, bread, and tea bags from the kitchen, and hiked back to Willow. There I started a pot of water on the hot plate, ate some of the cheese, took off my shoes, and flopped down on the bed, wondering what I thought I was doing there anyway, wishing for a pizza, and imagining myself telling the monks I wanted to go home now. I'd been there three hours so far.

Soon, out of desperation, I got up and started writing in my journal. For an hour, I kept a running catalogue of my thoughts, and I've recorded them here. The blank spaces are where I didn't write anything down.

1. What am I going to do with all this *time?*
2. Stop thinking about Joe and relax.
3. I don't think I'll ever be able to make Many Paths as special as this place.
4. How do they build these cabins? Maybe I should sketch one. [I sketched one.]
5. Damn. I didn't bring anything to read.
6. I wonder what Joe would be doing.
7. I'm not really bored. Just antsy.

8. Is it okay to waste time like this?
9. This is not wasting time.
10. Okay. But is it okay not to be *doing* anything?
11. Just try to *be.* No, don't try. Just *be.*
12. It's amazing how much I can write when I haven't got anything else to do.
13.

Here I stopped and ate some more cheese and a banana.

14. There's actually a chamber pot in here. But I don't think I'm going to use it because I don't want to wash it.
15. I seem to be slowing down a little, now.
16. Cheese gets boring.
17. So do bananas.
18. I hope nobody saw me put all that food in that sack.
19. This cabin is almost too nice.
20. I like mint tea.
21. At least a dozen people have sat in this chair and drunk hot tea because there are so many cup-size circles in the wood. [The arm of the chair was flat.]
22. What to do now? Think I'll read this journal.
23. Well, I read the journal. Now what?
24. Writing doesn't seem so much like work when you're not trying to finish something.
25. They shouldn't have this clock in here. It's too hard not to notice it.

26. That contact lens solution was five dollars! That little bitty bottle. My doctor has expensive taste.

27.

28. My ears ring in all this quiet.

29.

30. No bird sounds now. Where are they?

31. God, I'm lethargic. Probably too much cheese.

32. Slow down slow down slow down slow down slow down slow down slow down slow down slow down.

33. *Can I really stand four days of this?*

34. Quieter now but still restless. Think I'll go for a walk.

35. It's four o'clock.

36. Time flies.

37. The spaces between thoughts are longer now.

Early the next morning, I stepped onto the porch, headed for breakfast at the lodge, when I was surprised to find that it was snowing—those wide, heavy, perfectly formed flakes that make a soft *sshhh!* sound as they sift through the trees and plop onto the ground. It had been snowing for a long time, even though it was the end of March and temperatures had been mild. As I walked through the field, it seemed as though the vast new whiteness, the pale rocks in the creek bed that crossed the path, the bleached cottonwoods, the silver water in the pond down the hill all took on, or took in, light—took on brightness and warmth and a clarity I hadn't experienced since childhood. I found I had a whole day yet to hear the wind in the trees around my cabin, to take in the scents and textures of sky, field, and wood, to taste the apples I'd brought in my cooler, to sit on the porch of my hermitage and watch the night come in.

Now I live in, not those same woods, but woods all the same, in a cabin that seems far too large, by a pond that turns the color of copper at dusk on winter evenings. It's nearing the end of December and the maples on the banks have lost their reds and golds, but I saw two deer in the Dills' field this afternoon all tawny brown. I've got incense burning, and the air's full up with sandalwood and cedar. The space heater's keeping my back warm and I'm drinking my fresh-brewed coffee, watching the day draw down, thinking about the twenty-six pairs of shoes in my closet and wondering why I still need them.

*N*ot only do I own twenty-six pairs of shoes, but in preparation for moving to an even smaller cabin next summer I've given most of my furniture to my sister and I still have more chairs than I have pairs of underwear. I could sit in a different chair every day for three weeks. I have director's chairs, yellow-and-chrome dining room chairs, lawn chairs, a fishing chair, a boat chair, patio chairs, a cushy rattan chair with an ottoman from which I watch *Mystery!*, and a bamboo chair. I have no idea where they all came from. Of course, when I moved to the cabin I was supposed to scale down to the essential. But things keep accumulating. Last month I took a carload of my old clothes to a rescue mission and I still have thirteen pairs of jeans and I wear them all.

After I'd been living at the cabin for a while, a friend was looking around the place and she laughingly suggested that I had a tendency to collect things. I protested, explaining that I had rid myself of most of my material possessions before I moved from Kansas. Just because I had caches of arrowheads, rocks, feathers, baskets, shells, shark's teeth, beads, boxes, CDs, Chinese mud men, earrings, brass candlesticks, pottery, Indian blankets, and Christmas decorations didn't mean I wasn't managing to simplify as I had planned.

But today I'm counting and I'm forced to admit my friend was right. Books: six hundred and twenty-four. Boxes: two dozen. Shark's teeth: fifty-six. Seashells: many. Japanese teacups: two (both cracked). Pottery: seventeen pieces in various permutations. Baskets: I stopped collecting those.

Beads: several hundred. Arrowheads: eleven, not including the imperfect ones. CDs: I'm embarrassed to say. Feathers: seventy-nine, especially owl. Brass candlesticks: fourteen. Rocks: nine.

I was collecting homeless animals but that got too expensive.

 Thomas Merton wrote that everything you love for its own sake blinds your intellect and keeps you from knowing the way things really are, so I used to work hard on dropping my attachments, particularly to material things albeit obviously not to shoes, books, beads, feathers, brass candlesticks, and so forth. I used to give my things away. I tried not to discriminate between things that were valuable, either in terms of their expense or their importance to me, and things that were not. In fact, if I felt some attachment to them, I was that much more eager to get rid of them.

I gave away a Navajo bracelet, an antique sapphire-and-diamond ring that was a gift from my mother, a Mayan blanket from the Yucatan, a Cherokee drawing from Oklahoma, a sculpted eagle, a jade turtle, a Seneca dance rattle, a Portuguese box that I adored, an Egyptian scarab on a gold chain, a pair of Zuni earrings that I used to trade with my sister every other Christmas, an opal pendant my dad gave my mom, dozens of books, two arrowheads, and lots of other things I can still name. I gave these things on impulse to acquaintances in bars and strangers in libraries, a bit more thoughtfully to friends I knew well, relatives I knew less well. In my head is a catalogue of all these items side by side with the faces of the persons to whom they now belong—which has alerted me to the fact that simply giving a thing into another's keeping does not in the least sever my attachment to it.

*P*eople often ask me if I'm ever lonely. For a long time, I answered no. But the passage of that demon time in the form of years on end without intimate one-on-one human contact has forced me to acknowledge that I do experience moments of utter loneliness, despite the fact that I am surrounded by the essence of life that breathes in all living things. Late at night I fall asleep to the cries of coyote pups searching one another out in their dens. When I walk, the scent of pine, the sweetness of honeysuckle and the damp earth near the swamp, the musty perfume that clings to wet leaves after a rain catch me up and I pause on the path, unwilling to pass by such fragrances without taking them into me as I would enfold a lover. Even a neighbor's smile holds an enveloping warmth. These are the arms of God, one wise friend tells me, and I live within them. They carry me in all the spaces and times through which I pass, and I am never alone.

I am never alone, and the soul is never lonely, my wise friend says. But as much as I'd like to deny it, and as spiritually enlightened as I'd like to claim to be, I am not yet so in tune with my formless nature that I don't, like my dog Max, sometimes stick my psychic paw into the steel trap of this old body. A short woman with small wrists, blue eyes, and blond hair that has darkened as I've grown older, I'm as nearsighted as an armadillo and given to rambling. I am tangible reality, and whatever it is in my material nature that smells and touches and tastes and sees and hears also longs at times to connect with another tangible reality on the deepest level of our physical existence—to feel the warmth of a lover against my skin, to know a kiss that leaves me breathless, to possess that interlocking movement that only long and intimate relationship can bring, when passion admits no clarity but what hands touch and all sense is purest reason. When I find myself running one of my lonely stretches, it's usually after by accident I have found or by sheer determination I have dredged up a hint of this kind of intimacy with some friend and ended up rather unkindly reminding myself what close relations I've been giving over in order to lead my solitary life. It's not the not-having, really; it's the contrast between the rediscovered possibility of having and the reality of not-having that brings the loneliness into consciousness.

So my loneliness does not grow out of my solitude. It comes, rather, from my human longing to be gathered warm and close in human arms. Thoreau wrote that the value of a man was not in his skin, that we should touch him. But in my rare moments of loneliness, it is a human touch that I crave and from which all my spiritual ramblings have not the power to detach me. A familiar arm around my waist, a tender kiss on my bare shoulder: I have found no substitute for this.

tea mind

Tea is nought but this:
First you heat the water,
Then you make the tea.
Then you drink it properly.
That is all you need to know.

SEN RIKYU

I've been living at the pond for a long time now without hot water. People look at me with a kind of wonder when I tell them. One fellow asked me why I looked so clean.

People like to sit around and talk about the fact that I don't have hot water. I heard about some friends of mine who got hung up one day at lunch trying to figure out how I took a shower. They never could get it.

But they don't want me to tell, either. Like the friend who said that if I was fibbing about the hot water, he didn't want to know.

Now in a cabin without hot water, how hard the living is, or how easy, comes down to what a person gets used to. It's a way of life—same as air-conditioning, a nine-to-five job, children, or dogs.

But I'll admit that at first I did have to make some adjustments. I mean, when I wash the dishes, I have to heat water on the stove to wash them in. That takes time.

Same thing every night with the shower. I have to wait for the water to boil. That comes when it comes. It comes, as Robert Heinlein wrote, when the waiting is full.

I can't move very fast, either, while I'm carrying that tin pot full of boiling water those forty feet from the kitchen to the bathroom and then around two corners into the shower. I have to put one foot in front of the other. I have to move step by step. I have to glide, like a woman with a basket on her head. I can't think about where I'm going, I have to pay attention to where I am.

So this alternative showering does have its challenges, particularly in January. There's no heat at the cabin except what the space heaters generate, so to get the bathroom (the uninsulated bathroom with the window that doesn't meet the ledge) warm enough for a wet naked body, I have to let the space heater run in there for half an hour. Meanwhile, if I open the bathroom door, the rest of the cabin sucks out all the heat. What that means is that when the water boils, and I finally reach the bathroom door carrying that pot, I have to set the pot down, on the floor, and then open the door and pick up the pot and go inside really fast and hook the door with one foot and pull it shut (without spilling any of the water), and then put the pot on the floor of the shower, and then go back and shut the door. Then I take off my clothes and step into the shower—and I'm all set.

As the months drew on, I began to get accustomed to heating water on the stove. After a while, I was just carrying the pot, taking showers, heating water, washing dishes. I was what Keats wrote: a foster child of silence and slow time.

Then one night I stayed at my mother's house in town. The next morning, I went into the bathroom and twisted a knob and—*zap!*—out came hot water. A few minutes later, I was clean, dry, dressed, and sitting at the breakfast table, eating cheese eggs.

I once went backpacking for a week in Colorado. For six days, I carried everything I needed to survive on my back: place to sleep, clothes, food, water, knife, pen, book. Everywhere I went, I went on foot. I walked forty miles. It took a long time.

For six days, I never saw another human being. I never heard a car, never turned on a radio, never made a telephone call. I pitched my tent at dusk and built my fires, boiled my coffee in the mornings, cooked my breakfast. The sun was up, the sun was down. I walked, ate, made camp, read, wrote, slept, broke camp, and walked again.

Then the day came to go home. I hiked down out of the mountains to the road, where a car met me to drive me to the airport. The next thing I knew, I was racing down the highway, passing all these other people carrying backpacks. Then all of a sudden I was in the plane. Three hours later I was a thousand miles from the Colorado mountains, sitting on a sofa in Kansas, listening to the mulberry trees around my patio rustle in the breeze.

$\mathcal{H}$ot water from a tap is like that trip back to Kansas.

m o u s e

It was one of those damp, bone-chilling winter nights down south and this old scarecrow of a cabin was as cold as the family boneyard on the backside of Gene's rye field. The sixties-vintage space heater my dad had unearthed from his basement let out a feeble grinding noise, emanating little warmth and far too much light for three o'clock in the morning.

The temperature in the cabin hovered around forty. The draft from the windows had risen to a gale, and I was wide awake in the bed with my stomach in a knot, certain that the mice I could hear scratching around behind the paneling were building a bonfire with the wiring. I was thinking how the Dormineys had a cabin once, until a squirrel bit into their wiring—but at least the Dormineys weren't in the place at the time. Now I lay in bed wondering why I still hadn't bought a smoke detector.

But my cat Sport was not concerned, holding vigil at the end of the bed with her ears pricked up. Sport was not at all like Grace, that ladylike long-haired feline who permitted the mice to go about their business undisturbed. Sport was of that crew-cut variety of muscle-bound street cats, mostly black but for her white boots and a sinister scar across her mouth that gave her the look of a barroom brawler. Sport had no soft spot for mice. She went after them with the fervor of Ahab after Moby-Dick, only she was usually the one out front, leaping ahead of them just in time to cut off their escape routes. Then she batted them around until they gave up the ghost.

Now in the dead of a biting winter night, while I shivered in my unwarm bed, alert for the smell of ozone and a telltale drift of smoke from the electrical outlet, Sport was lying at my feet, on the lookout for unwary rodents, when I saw her bunch up like a jungle animal about to spring. Out came a fat white-footed mouse from behind the paneling. He sallied toward the kitchen in a mouse-waddle, his nose waving from side to side, sniffing for snacks.

Whap! Sling! Sport hit the linoleum in a forward glide and went sliding across the floor into the next room.

The mouse streaked for the sofa.

Sport managed a ninety-degree turn and slammed into the sofa leg. *Blam!* But she was tough. She thrust out a white boot and—*zoom!*—out came the mouse and darted past Sport under the table.

I chuckled and I cheered. "Go, mouse! Go, Sport!" I yelled from the bed. I wasn't about to get the broom. It was too cold out there.

Then . . . *zoom!*—dashed the mouse into the bedroom, headed for the ottoman, Sport close behind.

Then . . . *zoom!* Up to the windowsill.

Zoom! Down to the nightstand.

Zoom! Under the bed.

Under the bed.

Under the bed.

After that, the cabin went quiet. Sport lay hunched on the rug, watching the darkness under the bed, waiting. I slid as far under the covers as I could go and watched, too, for a while. Then I dozed off.

Then . . . *zoom!* Across my forehead went that mouse. Flushed me up out of that cover like quail and I made a beeline for the broom.

Sport and I chased the mouse into the bathroom, where he squeezed behind the litter box and ran away through a hole in the wall.

I could feel those mouse tracks on my head for days. When I went to bed at night, I closed my eyes and saw dozens of mouse feet making tiny impressions in the sheets.

There was a time after I moved into the cabin when I was without a cat. Sport, the bane of mousedom during her existence in this sphere, had been borne away by feline leukemia to torment mice in another dimension.

The result was that the community of rodents who had been going about their mousey business in the empty spaces behind the paneling, and having many late-night parties there, and building bonfires (I was certain) in the wiring, found themselves liberated. So they decided to take a hiatus from their cramped quarters and move out into the wide-open spaces of my den. Considering that my bedroom makes up the far end of the den, and the kitchen the opposite end, I would say that in the wake of Sport's demise the mice pretty much moved back in with me.

And these mice certainly considered me no enemy. They were only humoring me, peeping at me in the dead of night, chattering, giving me a chance to hurl an invective or maybe a shoe, so I could feel I was accomplishing something.

These mice, they had what I'd call a sanguine disposition. They were what I'd call unflappable. Sure, I took a few swipes at their heads with the broom, and sometimes I chased one into the bathroom—but my efforts never prompted them into much of a hurry. I didn't compel them to zoom. They only ambled and shambled barely fast enough to stay ahead of me, which isn't hard to do when you can squeeze under furniture.

And these mice, they had a crafty sense of knowing just when I had settled into some comfortable niche I'd be reluctant to vacate—such as under the blankets in the bed with a book on the coldest night in January.

After a while, I began to chafe under the bold, patronizing airs of these mice. I declared war. I went to the hardware store.

The hardware store was a mouse-catcher's paradise. They had those cardboard mouse-boxes with the superglue on the inside. They had those old-fashioned mousetraps with the slammers. They had those little blue pellets that make the mice thirsty so they go outside and drink water and die. Only they don't always go outside. Sometimes they go under the refrigerator.

I bought them all—all the lethal instruments, every variety. I bought some cheese. I bought some peanut butter. I'd heard stories about peanut butter from some friends of mine in Minnesota.

It took me a while but I set every one of those traps. I put peanut butter in half the traps and cheese in the other half. Then I sneaked around and slid the traps and little handfuls of blue pellets into all the mouse haunts in the cabin: behind the bookcase, behind the refrigerator, behind the stove, under the bathroom sink, between the sofa cushions, on the ledge by the kitchen window, inside the brass bowl with the pinecones. Then, like my cat Sport used to do, I waited. For days and nights on end, I waited. But nothing happened. No mouse stuck to the superglue, no mouse in the mousetrap, no mouse under the refrigerator.

Then one Saturday I left home on my weekend run to Wal-Mart and came back after dark. When I opened the cabin door, I heard a vague peep-and-shuffle coming from behind the bookcase. I turned on the light and pulled the bookcase out from the wall, and there I had one at last: a young white-footed mouse—a baby, really—in the old-fashioned mousetrap with the slammer. He was trying to pull himself free. The slammer had come down across his right shoulder where it met his neck, but it hadn't killed him.

Now, it was one thing to kill a mouse *in absentia*. It was another thing entirely to murder one with my bare hands.

I put on my work gloves and picked up the mousetrap and took it outside. I was going to let the mouse go. But when I set him free, he couldn't walk because all his bones had been crushed on one side. He could only push himself around in a circle, dragging his head. What to do?

I could feed him to the dogs, I thought. But that seemed so uncivilized.

I could throw him over the fence and let something else eat him. But he would linger.

I could crush his head with my bootheel. Never. I didn't have the nerve.

I decided to shoot him. Quick and painless, I thought.

I went back in and got Mr. Norman's six-shooter and loaded it with rat shot. When I came back, the mouse lay huddled at the base of the black cherry tree by the back steps, trembling from the strain of having pulled himself forward a few inches. I pointed the gun at him, but I couldn't pull the trigger at first because my hands were shaking.

It took three shots before I finally hit him. It took a fourth to finish him off.

After that, I declared a truce and hauled all the mousetraps to the dump.

lines from keats in late november

November has settled in at the cabin. Now, at last, the days have gone cool, and when the wind is out of the south comes that dark brown smell of overturned earth from the fields. Around the pond, the sweet gums and the maples have turned to orange and red, and wild grapevines weave through the branches like yellow garland. From my windows I can see leaves on the water from the dogwoods and white elms near the banks. The black cherry by my back steps has been bare since late September.

Along the paths where I walk the pastures and the open land, the gerardia and goldenrod and honeysuckle from October are gone, their purples and golds replaced by the silvers and tans of midautumn grasses. Deep in the wood, the scent of pine is on the air, and the deer are on the move: I can see their tracks on the trails.

At the cabin, life is calm. The tractors are gone from the fields. Donnie has tied down his yellow crop-duster for the winter. The dogs lie on the grass in the sun, near the boat, which is pulled up on the bank. Geese fly over, headed for Florida.

Yet summer holds. A single stalk of rattlesnake weed still blooms pale yellow by a pecan tree I know, and lavender asters linger at the edges of roads.

But the breeze carries a chill, and on overcast days, that fragrance that comes in on a rain is deeper somehow in November than in July, with a hint of spice, like cinnamon, or clove. In the evenings, while I'm working, my fingers grow cold, and I hold a cup of coffee in my hands to warm them.

So I've set up the space heater in the bathroom, and put away the big green fan, and folded the comforter over the end of the bed. I've put out my flannel pajamas and my old gray sweater with the hole at the collar from where it hung on a nail by the door last winter. The well water is too cold for washing dishes, so I've set a pot of wash water on the stove.

Now it's late, and evening is drawing down. Night's coming in dark and cold, and the stars are out. There's a half-moon over the water and a barred owl calling from the live oak near the west gate. The night air smells of woodsmoke, from fires in the dens of houses down the road. I'm wrapped in my red plaid robe, and in a few minutes I'll sit down in the big chair with a Dickens novel and a mug of blackberry tea. The cats are curled up in a corner of the sofa, the dogs on their blankets in the doghouse, the mice in their nests behind the paneling. And all is quiet under the pines as autumn gathers in.

There are some famous lines from a Keats poem over whose meaning scholars have been arguing for two hundred years. I've known the words all my life: my teachers used to repeat them. " 'Beauty is truth, truth beauty,'—that is all / Ye know on earth, and all ye need to know."

"What was Keats saying?" scholars ask. "What did he want us to see?"

But I trace paths through sweet gum, pine, and wheat-colored grasses in late November, and they move in me, all these blues, grays, greens, and ambers, shifting and deepening under the autumn sky. These hooded mergansers dipping for their supper, these belted kingfishers chasing each other across the water, these crows and mockingbirds and blue jays, they call. By the fallen oak is beaver sign: the dogs showed me. And the snowy egret keeps watch from the east end of the hollow, where the small bass hide in the reeds.

At dawn the mist comes gliding in like herons over the pond and dissolves into the light at midmorning. And the dogs roll in the grass. And the light glitters like crystal on the water where it ripples along banks warmed by the afternoon sun.

And the crickets sing at sundown, and the November sky is gold on the horizon. These are the things I know. They are a truth as plain to me as this grandfather of a fishing cabin is real, and they speak in voices clear and frank and pure, and their language is a poem. "We are the country," they say, "and we are dancing on the back steps of autumn."

two-stepping

Well, it's Valentine's Day and I'm feeling kind of lonesome and since I've got nobody to dance with, I'll tell about what it's like for a girl to go two-stepping and waltzing until way past midnight and then tuck the strands of her long blonde hair back under her Stetson and walk out tall and easy on her partner's arm under the summer moon and head for breakfast in the truck. And if it sounds like a country song, why, I believe that's just what it is. I like country songs, particularly when I'm feeling lonesome. Country songs have soul and they can make a person cry.

I never could stand country songs until I moved out west. They embarrassed me, all that whining and slide guitar, and me being musical it made me cringe when the voices went a hair flat. Listening to a country song before I moved out west was like watching a soap opera. I couldn't do that, either.

But all that changed in Kansas. Now I particularly like John and Jack on *Days of Our Lives* and, heck, I'm even listening to a country song right this minute. I'm listening to Randy Travis sing about how he's feeling like an old pair of shoes.

I mentioned I was musical and I was. I had a guitar, and when I was eleven I wrote a song about Billy the Kid and at the end of the song when Billy got shot by the sheriff I banged on the guitar to make it sound like a gunshot. My Aunt Liz thought that was great. She used to come over to MaRe's house and ask me to sing that song. She was especially fond of listening to me sing I'm Going to Leave Old Texas Now They've Got No Use for the Longhorn Cow and Oh Shenandoah I'm Bound to Leave You and Oh Give Me a Home Where the Buffalos Roam. But my Aunt Liz was a cowgirl herself because she had her own horses, so her coming over to hear me sing about cowboys made perfect sense to me.

It's funny that I grew up in love with Roy Rogers and Dale Evans and horses in particular, and Westerns on television like *Laredo* and *The Virginian* and *Bonanza*, because my family never owned any horses and when Dr. Tom offered to give me his big Tennessee walker named Carolyn Ann my folks wouldn't have any part of that—figuring they'd be the ones going out to the barn every night to feed her. They were wrong, but I was only ten at the time and how was I going to prove anything to a grown-up?

I had a crush on Trampas but Hoss Cartwright was

my dream husband. When I was a girl my first wish was to marry a Texas rancher. He'd be just like Hoss and we'd own a string of horses and have land that stretched as far as I could see like on *High Chaparral*. I wanted to get up at daybreak and go outside and feed the horses and the dogs and then come back in and make breakfast for the ranch hands. There weren't any trees on that ranch, only sagebrush and cactus and a lot of dirt, which I would rake into patterns in the yard.

When I was seven I used to go to the show with my next-door neighbor Sherry and we'd eat red hots and Sugar Babies and watch Roy Rogers double features. That was the year I got a Dale Evans outfit for my birthday and Pop gave me my first rod and reel, so sometimes I wore my Dale Evans outfit fishing because to tell the truth Mama didn't want me to wear it anywhere else. It had a skirt with fringe and a cowboy shirt and two silver six-guns. And a red hat with a string to pull tight under my chin.

I also wore my Dale Evans outfit to the rodeo on Sundays. We used to have rodeos all the time in Ocilla. The rodeo was out by the old prison camp, which wasn't abandoned at the time, so the prisoners could watch the rodeo through their cell bars. Made sense, to my mind— the outlaws and the good guys. But nobody ever busted out while I was there.

At the rodeo I got to ride a horse around the ring with all the other children, and if we didn't get scared and start crying we won the blue ribbon. I didn't see what there was to cry about: the cowboys led the horses and they refused to let go of the reins even if a person begged.

I had several blue ribbons on my bulletin board at home, but I was most impressed with my friend Dana because she had lots more ribbons than I did, and hers were all colors. But anyway I never got any cowboy boots until I was twenty-one.

A pair of Wrangler boots was the first thing I bought when I moved to Kansas. Went straight to the Western Duds store and bought a pair of palomino-colored leather Wrangler cowboy boots with pointy toes and inch-high heels. Since then I've had the big-name boots like the Justins and the Tony Lamas, and a pair of knee-high cowhide boots with the hair still on that looked pretty under a Western skirt, and I've had some decorator boots, too, with the silver tip on the toe and the brass chain around the ankle and the fancy tooling all up the sides. But none of them could hold a candle to those Wranglers. When I cleaned the cabin the night Grace got out, besides a pair of Justin Ropers those Wranglers were the only boots I kept.

But this isn't about boots, is it. It's about dancing. I'd argue, though, that the right boots make a difference in how the dancing comes out, because without the right boots a person can't get her balance. Her feet get tangled up or she slides around too much on the sawdust or her toes get to aching and then she can't do the steps right. She's got to do the steps right if she's going to dance. So she's got to have the right boots to dance in.

Now dancing. The first part of dancing is getting dressed up to go dancing. Besides boots, it's very important what a person wears because she has to dress like she knows how to dance. I mean, if she went to the Black Creek Saloon in her gym shorts and Nikes, even holding a long-necked beer bottle and leaning against the bar with her tennis-shoed foot cocked up on the bar rail could not make her look rangy and rough like she just rode in from Oklahoma. She's got to wear her Levi's—or now it's Wranglers. If she doesn't have Wranglers that are too tight in the butt or if they don't crumple up at the bottom because they're too long, she's not a real cowgirl. Because when she's sitting on her horse, her Wranglers have to come down over the tops of her boots. And if she's sitting on a barstool it's the same thing.

But I was two-stepping before the Wranglers turned high fashion, so for me it was Levi's. And a Western shirt is good, too. Long-sleeved. With a yoke across the back and snaps instead of buttons. And the belt has to match the boots and if a person had a string tie, that'd be okay, too. After that, it's all about the hat.

I had three hats—two Stetsons and a Resistol. I liked my straw Stetson best because it had curled up around the edges and had a leather strap around the brim with some hatpins on it—an armadillo and a pheasant. Like a fisherman wears lures on his cap, so does a cowgirl wear hatpins. But of course a person can't wear her straw hat in the winter, so my other two hats were felt, but they didn't have decorations because they were my dress hats.

Now, the hat can be a great attention-getter if a person is a girl and especially a southern girl and nobody knows what the girl really looks like until she takes off her hat and shakes out her long blonde hair and says something like, "Hey, y'all."

The hat is especially effective if the girl learns to do tricks with it, like flipping it over her wrist when she puts it back on. It's like twirling a six-gun around her fingers before she slips it into her holster. There's a certain fascination for the people watching. They say, "Hey, how'd you do that?"

It's a happy thing.

"Do that again," they say.

And then the music starts and that cowboy the girl's been talking to grabs her hand and says, "Come on, girl. Let's go dance."

So the girl steps out onto the dance floor holding hands with a stranger and he puts an arm around her waist and pulls her close and takes an easy step or two in time to the music to see if she can follow, and she does, she follows perfectly, and she remembers that this is the part she came for. Step, step, wait; step, step, wait. He moves, she moves with him. He lifts her hand, she dips under and turns, smooth, on her toes, easy, the balls of her feet just touching the floor, and he smiles because she is graceful and this is natural. Like fishing. Not something she has to think about, but something that's born into her. They're an entity. They cohere. He moves, she moves. He lifts her hand again and this time he dips, deeper than she does because he's taller and she can't reach as high, and he spins and does a fancy step, and she smiles to show she appreciates it. Step, step, wait; step, step, wait. Around and around, down and turn. And that's two-stepping.

And afterward they have the dance between them. So maybe later they waltz, or they do the Cotton-Eyed Joe. It doesn't matter. They're just dancing.

And then it's last call and she tucks the strands of her hair back under her hat and they walk out into the night. She holds on to his arm, leans against him a little. It's summer and there's a moon, and they stand on the driveway for a few minutes, taking in the quiet. They talk in whispers. A couple comes out the door of the saloon behind them and the noise from inside—laughter, a name called, bottles clinking, barstools scraping across wood floors—the noise from inside fills the air and then is gone.

They decide to take his truck to Sly's for breakfast, come back later for hers. His truck is big, roomy, with a long bed on the back and a winch on the front, and he opens her door for her and she climbs in and slides to the middle. Inside, the air smells like leather. His work gloves are on the dash, the case with his sunglasses over the visor. As he pulls out of the driveway she turns around and looks back. He notices, and as he turns onto the road he puts his arm around her shoulders, and he leaves it there, all the way to Sly's.

walking the lines

I was sitting on the steps with my coffee this morning, watching the pond water ripple under the breeze, and I was wondering where the golden cord is that ties this land to me.

Ownership: it's nothing you can touch. The only thing that connects me to this spring-clear water, this wild wood with its changing leaves and yellow vines is the words on a paper down at the courthouse with some names and a date on it.

"You're my dog," I tell Max. I wonder if he thinks he's mine.

"These are my blueberry bushes," I tell my friends in

summer. "Have some of my wild blackberries. Take some of my pinecones home with you."

"I'm borrowing your shovel," I tell Gene. He paid money for it; that makes it his. But I don't see any shimmering thread attaching that shovel to his heart. If I told people that shovel was mine, they'd never know the difference.

It comes down to money, to some kind of trade. My great-grandfather paid money for these fields, these sweet gums and blowing grasses. But it's Gene who for fifty years has built a life out of what he has coaxed from these fields he has leased from my family, and that's his son Donnie who now flies the yellow crop-duster from the airstrip they've mowed on the hill, and that's Donnie's son who now runs down to the pasture with his grandmother to help feed the new calf. So what's a fair price for so many lives made? And which one of us has paid it?

What would the market bear, I wonder, for four hundred acres of autumn? For the sound of leaves rustling outside a cabin window? The crunch of pine needles underfoot? The smell of peanuts drying in a field? For deer and owl and coyote?

Or what can you trade for summer? For toes dug into soft mud at the edge of a pond and the thrill when your red-and-white plastic bobber darts downward? For a boat slipping quiet across water, the knock of paddle against gunwale? Blackbird, whippoorwill, and bullfrog?

Easier to price winter, maybe, and freezing nights, bare oaks, gray skies. The way ice forms around the edges of puddles. The north wind, whistling in cracks where cabin windows don't quite meet the ledge. The way you shiver when you leave your warm blankets for the morning.

Mice behind the bookcase, coming in from the cold.

But we'll find out soon enough. The signs are up: my relations are selling the farm.

$\mathcal{W}$hen I was a child my dad and I were driving to Florida and I asked him to show me the state line. I expected to see a break in the earth or a long hump of dirt showing me where Georgia ended and Florida began. When we drove over the state line on the highway, he said, "This is it, Amy. This is the line." But I couldn't see anything but pavement. I couldn't even feel a bump. If it hadn't been for the Florida welcome center, I'd never have known we weren't in Georgia any more. The scenery looked the same to me.

My dad explained that the boundaries between the states were imaginary, but they were represented by lines drawn on a map. They only work, he said, because people agree to take them on faith. When people start disputing where to draw the lines, he said, you get wars.

I'm fascinated with the idea that the only thing separating Arizona from Mexico, say, or Georgia from Florida, or Pop's land from the part he sold to the Harpers twenty years ago is a line I can trace with my finger on a political map. On the National Geographic map of the physical world, there are no lines—only mountain ranges and deserts and rivers that go where they go.

There's another kind of boundary, though, that does have substance. Physical objects, tangible things, are divided by their edges from what they're not. My body, for instance, has its skin, an edge that holds my bones together in a measurable space and separates inside from outside.

The black cherry tree by my steps has its bark, which renders "tree" into a shape I can call by name.

But is what my physical eyes see all there is to that black cherry tree? Is what I see essence of tree, or do I see only a boundary, a kind of line drawn on a map for me to navigate by? "O chestnut tree, great rooted blossomer, / Are you the leaf, the blossom or the bole?" Yeats wrote. Certainly there is more to me than my outline in a mirror. So "black cherry tree" must also exist in the space beyond my vision.

And if that is so, then my skin has no real power to separate me from what isn't me, nor is black cherry tree truly defined, or confined, by the outline of its bark. Like the M. C. Escher lithograph where the hands emerge out of the page and draw themselves: you can't quite put your finger on the line that separates the hand drawing from the hand drawn. "How can we know the dancer from the dance?" wrote Yeats.

Sometimes at night I sit out here on the steps and stare not at the stars but at the spaces between them. I try to imagine the whole of the universe, how far beyond my vision it must extend. But no matter how hard I try, I can't hold the idea of infinite space in my mind. I can only get my imagination around finite ideas, ones that have edges my mind can trace, like Moon. Heron. Pond.

Except once. I was lying in bed one night, wishing I could sleep, when I suddenly found myself speeding through a dark tunnel that opened into outer space. At the end of the tunnel I could see stars, tiny points of light sparkling far off in the black void of the cosmos. I knew that when I reached the end of the tunnel I would race out into that place, that I would be in space. An instant later, I did fly out the end of the tunnel ... but I was not in space, after all. I *was* space. I was nothing; I was the void. I was the blackness between the stars, and all the stars were within me. I was "pure sensation unencumbered by meaning," as Annie Dillard wrote. Then I was back in my bed, wishing I could sleep.

For me, the space between the stars is like negative numbers. Negative numbers seem to me like inversions of positive space, like black holes. On the other hand, to imagine the largest number is like trying to apprehend infinity and I'm back to the space between the stars again.

It's like physics. I can't stand to think about nanotechnology: the size of the parts drives me to distraction. Chemical factories, machines, whole computers the size of molecules and *smaller*—how could anyone have dreamed up such a thing? I imagine tiny technicians wielding screwdrivers the size of neutrons, wee analysts writing wee programs with wee pencils. That's how limited my imaginative power is when it comes to anything so far beyond my frame of reference. Thinking about nanotechnology feels like ants picking at the edges of my brain.

But the Zen masters tell me that if with single-minded attention I ponder a puzzle that has no solution—infinite space, the surface of a Möbius strip, the sound of one hand clapping—out of sheer confusion the cup of my mind will empty and I will encounter the I AM, I will move beyond the beyond, transcend the boundary between the form and the formless. *Zap!* Enlightenment. The cup is filled. "It is a sort of mental catastrophe taking place all at once," said D. T. Suzuki, "after much piling up of matters intellectual and demonstrative." So perhaps I should not mind the ants.

Time is another concept to which I've ascribed boundaries that don't really exist. I measure time by events. First one thing happens, then the next. Seconds pass from one tick to the next tick, and minutes, hours, days, eons drag by. But my veterinarian tells me that animals have no sense of time. If I leave Max and Queenie with him for three weeks, to me it's three weeks because I maintain a linear notion that the event of my returning happens after the event of my leaving and that the passage of time is the link between the two events. This leaves me vulnerable to all kinds of anxieties associated with the idea of time as linear—nervousness over being gone so long and, toward the end, impatience to get back. But to Max and Queenie, says my vet, they're just at the kennel, and I'm not. Then I'm there and we're going home. They have no sense of in-between: they know only the moment they inhabit.

God is like time, I think. What boundaries I have ranged around God are all imaginary. Krishnamurti said that the creative state is God. But the ancients say that a god defined is a god confined. That is, to propose an idea of God narrows the mind and excludes the greater fact.

So the imaginary lines I draw around God to create my image of God limits God to the image my intellect is capable of creating. When I consider the narrow scope of my mind, how poorly I score on reading comprehension tests and how it discomfits me to think about the indefinite, or the limitless, then I consider that my ability to imagine God must be very small. A Catholic priest once told me that I must not try so hard to put my arms around God, that I should allow the outlines of God to remain fluid. I have to become satisfied with the not-knowing, he said, and that's a matter of faith. As Paul wrote to the Hebrews, faith is a belief not based on the evidence of the senses but on the evidence of things *not seen*. Believing that space extends past the limit of vision: that's faith.

Nevertheless, I do go looking for God—for God sign, like a good tracker. I look for it on the trails, listen for it in the cries of the great blue heron who lives on the pond. I know it must be there: Emerson said so. He said that this was nature's noblest ministry, to stand as the apparition of God. "It is the organ through which the universal spirit speaks to the individual," he wrote, "and strives to lead the individual back to it." And sometimes, in the change of light at sundown from pale blue into rose, in the image of a hawk spiraling upward on a thermal, in the perfection of a flint point that has lain undiscovered for a thousand years, I fancy I've found God sign, discovered the evidence of something I long to see clearly. Finding it difficult to be content with the not-knowing, I cling to what I can know.

There's a place I know on the other side of the dam where when it rains too much, the pond water rushes out in a wide stream and falls down a hill into a creek that bears it away to the Harpers' pond and then to the Willacoochee River. The dam doesn't hold the water in: the pond goes where it goes. My grandfather built that dam, just as my great-grandfather bought the right to claim this land for a while. But that word *ownership* holds no more real power than Pop's dam holds back the pond water when it gets too high. Ownership is only a bargain people make with each other, an idea that everybody takes on faith. It's a line on a map.

This place is more than what's held in by fences. I don't like the thought of its being sold, but selling it can never diminish whatever old loves still connect me to it. Old loves have nothing to do with lines, boundaries, ownership. And if there is any golden cord that ties me here, it will hold; for it lies out there in the woods, where when I walk the sound of the wind in the oaks plucks some deep harmonizing string in my own being. Or it hangs near this porch step, shimmering in some dimension I can't see, while I sip my steaming coffee and watch the reflections of November light sparkle and move away across the water.

squirrel shooting

$\mathcal{I}$ was never much of an athlete, but I'm comfortable outdoors and my constitution is strong, and I like to play at staying in shape, so I've always thought that as long as I could keep my wits about me I'd be able to handle myself if the circumstances got rough.

The problem is, most of my friends are experts at some kind of athletic activity and they all like a sporting challenge. One pair of six-foot Minnesota friends, for instance, spend their summers taking steps three at a time to stay in shape for cross-country skiing, which is in season up there for most of the year. So I did my first cross-country skiing in northern Minnesota in a forty-below wind chill on a trip that began before breakfast and ended after supper. I don't know how many miles we went but it was many. I was the last one back to the lodge and it took me a week to teach my two-and-a-half-foot-long legs how to move again. It was like trying to walk on solid ground after roller-skating all night—or like stepping off an escalator over and over and over again.

I spent the longest week of my life backpacking with Terry over a Wyoming mountain range in the snow, trying to follow the cut marks on the trees. He always did like adventure, so he decided to take us down the advanced backpacker's trail. But my sense of balance is not too keen, and I almost slid eleven thousand feet down a mountain on an avalanche. I almost fell down a washed-out riverbank into a waterfall, almost sank through a beaver dam into an ice-covered lake, and almost dropped our topographical map into a raging stream I was crossing on a fallen tree while carrying a sixty-pound pack on my back. I was almost swept downriver in a flood, almost blown away in a windstorm, and almost starved from developing a revulsion to Grape Nuts, powdered milk, and freeze-dried chicken hot pot.

That was the first day. After that, all I could think about was pizza. When we got back to our rented truck a week later, our wallets were almost ruined from lying in the snow on the open tailgate, where I had left them.

I might have learned something from that experience. But I had a retired friend who competed in biathlons and he taught me how to cycle on a ninety-mile ride that began after breakfast and ended before lunch. I spent the next three days soaking in Epsom salts and eating bananas.

The second time I tried that ride, I slid down in a puddle in a parking lot and spent the next three days in the hospital. I was recovering from four hours of surgery on the ankle I had broken into so many pieces that it took two steel pins, a nail, two plates, and seventeen screws to put it back together again. I'm still paying the doctor.

After my ankle healed I went camping in an Arizona desert in February with a sleeping bag rated for August. Then I tried to ski down a double-diamond slope at Breckenridge and had to be rescued by a snowmobile.

I've canoed the White River in northern Arkansas during a spring flood, water-skied too fast somewhere in Florida, and scuba-dived too deep for too many minutes in the Missouri Ozarks. I've been thrown off horses barrel-racing in Georgia and scraped off horses by low-hanging branches in eastern Kansas. I've knocked my shoulder out of joint from shooting Terry's twelve-gauge shotgun out the front window of his Chevrolet Suburban, road-hunting during an Oklahoma ice storm. But somehow I've survived rabbit hunting, pheasant hunting, quail hunting, and squirrel hunting without visible scars.

One overcast day, Terry was teaching me how to hunt small game when he pointed to a deadfall and whispered that there was a rabbit on the other side. I crept around the edge of the deadfall, but I was too noisy and the rabbit got away.

Then Terry saw a squirrel. But before I could aim the Browning, the squirrel ran up a tree. He had a nest at the top. I could see his tail sticking out over the edge of the nest, so I shot him. Shot him right out of the nest. He landed at Terry's feet.

"Blooded at last," I said, picking up the squirrel by the tail and holding him aloft like a prize marlin.

Terry frowned at me. "You're not supposed to shoot them out of the nest," he said.

"Why not?"

"It's not fair," he said.

That seemed absurd, considering I was the one holding the shotgun.

We headed out to find more game. Terry wouldn't put the squirrel in his game bag. "It's your kill," he said. "You carry it."

I didn't have a game bag, so I had to carry the squirrel by the tail. He kept slipping because his fur was long and soft and he was heavier than I thought he'd be. This bothered me. One minute, eating acorns; next minute, dead weight. I didn't shoot anything else.

At home, I had a wild game cookbook and I was determined to eat the squirrel for supper. I skinned him— it's not as hard as people say—and picked out most of the shot. I soaked him in vinegar and water for a long time, then cut him up for squirrel and wild rice stew.

I crockpotted that stew for hours, but the meat never did get tender, and I couldn't get rid of that wild taste. Finally I threw the whole thing in the trash. I gave the Browning away.

*N*ow every day I go out hunting down through April field and southern wood, with my walking stick of South Carolina hickory to nudge the snakes out of my path. This afternoon, after some bean soup and a glass of sweet tea, I'm going to leave behind the fat red-bellied woodpecker who's been hammering at the water oak behind the cabin and see if I can find the cottontail who leaves his footprints by the creek. The dogs will chase their armadillos, and maybe I'll catch sight of the gopher turtle in his den at the edge of the Dills' cotton field. Maybe we'll see deer and coyote, and the fish hawk who lives at the alligator pond, where the beavers are burrowing under the dam. On the way, I'll stop and whistle to the red-winged blackbirds, and taste the honeysuckle growing thick and sweet along the fence.

In the forest, the wisteria is gone, but the dogwoods and wild cherries and chinaberries are blossoming now, and on the way to the swamp I know a sandy clearing rimmed by live oaks draped with Spanish moss and ivies that twine in easy ribbons through the trees. It's a good place to sit and think on a warm late-April morning, to listen to the crows caw in the cypresses, and watch the squirrels chase each other through the sunlight.

r u n n i n g

The late-August afternoon was far too hot for running and the red dirt road was rocky and dry. The dogs had gone home after we'd reached the first-mile curve when they saw that I intended to keep going. I was trying my first six-mile run.

There was no competition involved: six miles was only a personal goal. I'd never even run four miles before that summer, and when I found out I had it in me to run four, I thought I might be able to run six, roughly ten kilo-meters. Biathlon distance. I liked to think I'd be able to finish a biathlon, though I had no plans to try. I just wanted to know I could do it.

Now I'd just made the turnaround at the three-mile branch and was coming back over a culvert that drained into a narrow creek bed waterless from weeks without a good rain. Keeping to the road's edge, I tried to find flat dirt, away from the sandy ridges pushed up by the tires of passing trucks. I took a swallow of water from the bottle I was carrying and pressed the sweat out of my eyebrows with the backs of my hands.

The road was dry, but the humidity made the air feel like wet rags and there was no breeze except what I created as I pushed on. The bandanna around my forehead was soaked through, and sweat from my hair was dripping down the back of my neck. My clothes had been damp by the time I'd walked the half-mile to the plum trees at the end of Gene's driveway, where I started my runs. Now, as I struggled past the three-mile point, I started my usual battle with myself over whether to keep running or stop and gulp down the rest of my water and walk the dusty miles back home.

The three-mile point on a run has always marked my moment of inner conflict. It's that flashpoint where, like Donnie in his crop-duster heading down a field toward a line of trees, I have to make the all-or-nothing decision, where I believe I *must* stop or my body will collapse. By the time I reach the three-mile point, I've begun to feel every stitch in my knees and every jabbing pain from the old wound of my broken ankle. My shoulders ache and my breathing is too shallow and my legs are too tired. I long to be submerged in a mountain lake or sitting on the steps of the cabin drinking iced tea out of a clear glass. At the three-mile point, I'm mad that I'm running, and I'm mad that I want to stop running.

After the culvert over the creek bed there's a long stretch of straight road bordered on either side by pastures dotted with pecan trees. As I ran by an old well under a spreading pecan, I was looking toward the end of the road, where it sloped downward and out of sight. The sky seemed wide there and, that day, the width of sky made me think of eastern Kansas and a bicycle ride I used to make often, northward down a gravel road that ran between fields and fields of wheat.

The narrow Kansas road did not slope downward out of sight but rather stretched for over a mile up a long, steep grade. Cyclists called that hill by nasty names, and for novices like me, who did not possess those rock-hard cyclist's legs or bikes with gears that ground down into the negative numbers, a ride up it meant getting off halfway and pushing your bike to the top, which was a feat that for every inch was as grueling as staying in the saddle.

Running on Georgia dirt in late August, I was remembering the day I rode that Kansas hill in August once, alone. I wanted to see if I could get all the way to the top without walking. Kansas had its days reminiscent of Georgia summers, and the afternoon I made that ride, both the humidity and the temperature had topped out near a hundred.

The hill was a challenge partly because of its approach from down that long, straight road. There was no downhill stretch where I could get a running start—I'd have to come at the hill with only what speed my bare strength could find. After that, the rest of the climb would be sheer effort—or sheer determination. The last third of the way up, the grade suddenly intensified. If I couldn't ride it—which I'd have to do by standing on the pedals, no matter how low my gears would go—then walking and pushing would be about the same as carrying my bike up a kitchen staircase.

But I was in pretty good shape back then, and I had a good bike—an old Schwinn touring bike heavier than anything made now—and my three water bottles were full. So I pedaled down the straightaway and concentrated on the road ahead and told myself that no matter how exhausted I got, no matter how my shoulders ached or my legs burned, I would not stop.

The first third of the hill winded me, but not badly. I tried not to look too far ahead and kept going.

The second third was more of a struggle, especially with the high humidity. I was breathing hard, my knees were aching, and I was already down to my lowest gear.

I can't do this, I thought.

Keep trying, I argued.

I absolutely cannot do this, I thought.

The words went through my mind with every rotation of the wheels: *I can't do this. Keep trying. I want to stop. You can't stop. No. Yes. No.* They were my mantras.

The grade steepened. I inched up the hill. I pushed the pedal down; the bike shot forward and stopped. I pushed the other pedal down; the bike shot forward and stopped.

I can't do this. This is crazy.

Keep trying.

No.

I reached a place where I could see the top of the hill, although it was still a quarter-mile away. There, the road leveled out to a slight rise, then curled around to the west for five hundred feet until it began a gradual descent down the other side. That was when I saw what a fraud I'd been perpetrating on myself.

Because they were all, like "ownership," words without meaning. They were shapes without substance: "I can't do this; try; no." Buying into all that *effort*, that was the deception. There I was, pushing down those pedals, cycling up that hill on the hottest afternoon of the year, thirsty and tired and struggling. But was I trying? No. I was *doing*. I was riding, and I was climbing. If I'd gotten off my bike, I wouldn't have been climbing. There was no effort to it: it was only doing and not-doing. Yoda had said it years ago—"There is no try!" he said. Now, I was living it.

I did get off my bike that day. I got off it, in fact, right after I learned about doing and not-doing, and pushed my bike the rest of the way. And no matter how many times I rode that hill afterward, I never could ride to the top.

On a Georgia dirt road in August, though, the memory of that bike ride took me straight through the three-mile doldrums and I finished those six miles, and I kept running six miles for the rest of the summer—but I've never done it since. As I said, I've never been much of an athlete. I haven't got the discipline. So my tilts in athletic directions are only play. But they do keep me out-of-doors, where I can learn the shapes of words and recall the width of the sky.

lizards on the windshield

*O*n the way to Valdosta down Highway 135, there's a wooden sign in front of a trailer that sits on the north end of a round pond half the size of this cabin. On the bank of the pond is a folding chair. A chicken coop monopolizes a corner of the back yard, and in late summer a profusion of primroses crowds the front yard near the steps. As I pass, a brown dog with a doleful expression watches out from the porch.

The wooden sign sits beside the road. The top half, a faded gray, is a plywood cutout of a long, thin fish. The fish has no discernible character but for its top fin and a tail and the pouting shape of its mouth. Suspended beneath the fish by two thin chains is a white sign that bears a single word. The word is printed in black letters in a thin, childlike scrawl.

As I drove toward the sign with the fish on top, before I saw the word underneath, I thought the people who lived in the trailer must be growing fish in their pond, and the sign was an advertisement. An image came to mind of an old man sitting all day in the folding chair beside the pond, catching fish to sell to passersby. So I was surprised to find that the word on the sign was not about fish at all and that I'd had everything wrong—the fish, the old man in the folding chair, even the chicken coop in the back yard, which was not for chickens. Because the word on the sign was "RABBITS."

While I was driving to Ocilla one morning I became frustrated by an oak leaf flapping on the windshield, caught beneath the wiper blade. I pulled over beside a tobacco field, yanked up the parking brake, and glanced at the windshield again to discover not an oak leaf, after all, but a green anole. He was hunkered down, having worn himself out with the effort of keeping himself from being blown away in the blast of wind I'd created as I sped down the road at seventy-five miles an hour. I got out of the car and reached for him carefully, but as soon as he saw my hand he darted off in another direction. I chased around the car after him, feeling ridiculous as he raced from one side of the windshield to the other and time after time my hand came down on bare glass. A pickup driver tapped his horn at me as he went by; I saw him wave as he disappeared around a curve. Finally, the anole leapt off the windshield and ran away in the grass.

One Saturday I was on the way to Americus for my weekly visit with MaRe. It was ninety miles to Americus, so as usual I'd started out early, and the pale blue spring day was clear and warm. I still had my truck then, and it was noisy, but every time I slowed for a turn or a traffic light I heard birds chirping over the sound of the engine. Anyway, I went on.

When I reached Americus I pulled in at the mall, because I wanted to pick something up at Belk's before I went to the Magnolia Manor. As soon as I opened the truck door, I heard the birds again, and then it dawned on me that I had somehow brought them with me from the pond.

The chirping led me toward the tailgate, so I crawled under the back of the truck. There they were: three baby birds, along with two unbroken brown-flecked eggs, in a nest tucked inside the curl of the back bumper. Somehow they had all survived ninety miles of bumps and exhaust fumes.

I knew they'd never make it through a whole day of around-town driving and the trip back home to Lax that night. So when I saw the three children come out of Belk's with their mother, I hurried toward them with the nest. I begged them to try to raise the birds themselves. When I left the boy—he might have been eight years old—in the front seat of his car, cradling the nest in his lap, he was delirious with happiness. His mother was not.

The sky was dark gray one late summer afternoon and I was racing toward the cabin in the car, trying to make the front gate before the deluge. As I rounded a corner still five miles from home, a ray of sunlight shot out from between two clouds. I put on my sunglasses and was surprised to see not just gray sky but a broad, vivid rainbow, one of those perfect arcs without any gaps. It started near the cabin, I thought, and ended in Gene's back yard.

But the clouds soon obscured the sunlight, so I took my sunglasses off again, because the sky was too dark for me to see with them on. When I took off the sunglasses, the rainbow disappeared. I put them back on: rainbow. I took them off: no rainbow. Until I put on my sunglasses, I had believed the sky was only gray.

*T*hat the sun sinks is illusion: the earth spins backward, away from the sun. I once watched the sunset until I saw that this was true.

*C*oming home late one night, I watched a neon-blue meteorite float across the sky directly over the hood of my car and drop into the field behind the Dills' house on the paved road a half-mile east of the cabin. I went looking for it the next day, but I couldn't find anything. An astronomer told me later that the meteorite was really at least sixty miles away.

*A*nother reason I believed my cousin when she told me we could dig to China was that she ate raw ants. We were out at the cabin one day, playing by the pond, when she reached down and picked up an ant and popped it into her mouth. I couldn't believe it, so I made her do it again. She liked the way they crunched, she said. They didn't taste like anything, she said. She said people in France ate chocolate-covered ants all the time as a delicacy.

I couldn't imagine anybody eating ants and I refused to try it. But it's thirty years later and now I have friends who eat earthworms. Grubs, too. What can I say? I shrug and take another bite of sushi.

I did eat something that took me by surprise once, but it wasn't of the bug or worm persuasion. We were in a Chinese restaurant, this Thai friend of mine and I, and he challenged me to try a new food, something my palate had never experienced before. I agreed, but privately I thought it would be impossible. I couldn't imagine a taste that wouldn't ring somehow familiar. Any Anglo-Saxon who had learned to like sushi couldn't be in for much of a surprise, I thought, and besides, I'd been to Europe in my teens, and I'd been in Georgia and Minnesota and Wyoming and New Mexico, and I'd tasted the cuisines of dozens of different countries from South America to Thailand. Nothing could exist that was so radically different from all the other foods I'd eaten that I wouldn't be able to say "Well, that tastes like chicken," or "Well, that's kind of fishy," or "That tastes vaguely like something I ate in Oklahoma once"—something like that.

So the Chinese waitress set in front of me a bowl of small white balls. I frowned and poked them with a chopstick. I'd heard about people in Greece eating sheep's eyes and I wasn't keen on the idea.

But these white balls were fruitlike to look at. They had a strange consistency—kind of soft, but springy.

"What do they taste like?" I asked.

"Just try it," said my friend.

"Are they sweet?"

"Kind of."

"Will I like it?"

"Probably."

"Are you sure?"

I told my friend that when I was a kid I hated English peas. They made me gag. The first time I tried them, somebody told me they were kind of sweet and that I'd like them. I still pick them out of vegetable soup. If I get them on my plate by accident, I can't let them touch the potatoes.

I picked up one of the white balls. "Does it taste like English peas?" I asked.

"No."

"What do you call it?"

"Longan."

"Oh."

I closed my eyes and put the ball into my mouth, leery of biting down. When I did, the longan burst onto my tongue with a cloying, fruity sweetness. But this was a sweetness, a flavor, I had never known. I could compare the taste to nothing. It was, after all, entirely outside my experience. It was even, I realized, outside my capacity to have imagined. In its strangeness, I saw at once the bold outlines shaping my perception.

alligator moccasins

Nestled among the pines on the way to the swamp, about two miles from here down an old logging trail, lies the alligator pond. Donnie started calling the place the alligator pond in the seventies, because every time he flew over it he saw alligators in the water and on the banks.

I walk by the alligator pond often and look for alligators, but I've never seen one there. In fact, in all my years around the swamps of South Georgia, until I moved to the cabin I had never seen an alligator that wasn't on television. Even though old Johnny claimed he had seen one in our pond when he was fishing, as far as I know, no one else ever did. So it came as a surprise to me when, standing on the bank with the dogs one late-summer afternoon, I saw an alligator by the drain.

Since I'd never seen an alligator, I didn't realize it was an alligator I was seeing, at first. Its snout was out of the water, but only enough to resemble a big turtle head. But the more I looked at it, the more of it I saw, and when it occurred to me that I might have an alligator in the pond I panicked and ran inside to call Gene. He drove Alice and their daughter and her fiancé over here in the truck to have a look.

The sun was almost gone, and the rose-colored evening air was alive with mosquitoes, which made it hard to concentrate, and my hands were sweating from the September heat and Pop's old binoculars were foggy. Nevertheless, none of us had any doubt that it was an alligator we were squinting at, and an alligator who was squinting back at us. Maybe it was because of the dogs, standing on the banks, or maybe the alligator wanted one of us—but during the half hour the five of us passed around the binoculars and pointed at the alligator and talked nervously about what to do, she brought her whole six feet up to within two shovel-lengths of where we were standing. And there she floated—waiting, perhaps, for one of us to walk on into the water and get it over with or just leave so she could go back to her turtle supper. That was fine by me. We had too many turtles in the pond, anyway. They ate the fish. So turtles, frogs, snakes—whatever that alligator wanted, she was welcome to, as long as it wasn't dog legs, the neighbors, or me.

The next day I called the fish and game people. They would send out a couple of trappers, the ranger said, but

I'd have to wait until they could work me into their schedule.

"Alligators is partial to little gray dogs," the ranger said after I described Max. "Don't nobody know why. You say you got a dog pen? Well, I seen a gator climb a six-foot fence to get a dog one time. Gators is crazy when they're hungry. Don't you go near the water, now. Particularly not at night."

"No," I said. As if I would.

"See, a gator hunts at night," he went on. "How you can tell if you got you one is, if you shine a flashlight at him, his eyes'll light up like taillights."

Like the eyes of a jack-o'-lantern is what he should have said, and I could spot them all the way across the pond while, safe behind the screen door, I scanned the water with the flashlight. Slow as an old snapping turtle that alligator would cruise around the pond in the dark, her eyes glowing just above the water as she watched the banks. She was magnificent. She was a neon-eyed monster straight out of a Stephen King novel.

"See what a gator does is," the ranger had enlightened me, "he waits until a dog or something comes right up to the edge of the water. Then he goes after him. Then he stuffs him under a log and waits for him to rot."

I locked Max and Queenie in the cabin at night and in the dog pen during the day, hoping the pond's too many turtles would keep the alligator from climbing the fence for a bite of little gray dog.

The two trappers showed up around ten o'clock one night several weeks later with a bag full of rotting rattlesnakes in the back of a pickup. They'd use the snakes to bait the trap, they said, in case they couldn't catch her.

Catch her? I thought. Right.

And to my horror, they set off on the pond in a bass boat with nothing but their wits, their considerable brawn, their flashlight, and two long poles with nooses attached to the end—but not, thank heaven, with a boatload of ripe alligator bait.

For two hours, they chased the alligator around the pond. They'd creep up behind her, and she would speed off to the opposite shore. They'd reach out a pole, and she'd dive under. Finally, around midnight, they paddled back to the bank, where I was sitting on the tailgate of their truck, watching. One of them reached for the bait.

"Gonna have to set the trap," he said. "We'll come back and check it in a few days."

Away they went across the water with their fragrant rattlesnakes.

After a while, I heard them coming back. They had almost made it to shore when they spotted the alligator. She had come up onto the bank near the truck and was lying not that far from where my legs were dangling.

The next thing I knew, one of the trappers had slipped a noose around her snout and was standing in thigh-deep water, wrestling with her as she thrashed. The other trapper grabbed her tail, and soon her jaws were taped shut and her legs were taped behind her back and she was immobilized. Then she was in the back of the pickup, and then she was gone.

If it hadn't been for the dogs, I would have liked to keep that alligator. It was interesting, having an alligator in the pond. But then I wouldn't have the blue herons or the ducks or the otter, and maybe not the kingfishers, and certainly not the turtles. Probably not too many snakes. The fishing wouldn't be as good, either, or as safe. Alligators don't crawl into the boat while you're not looking; they wait for you to fall out, or maybe dangle your toes in the water. They're subtle, wrote the adventurer William Bartram after an alligator rushed at him from the reeds on the Altamaha River in 1770. Subtle, he said, but greedy.

But I've often wondered what happened to the alligator who found refuge in our pond for a while—if those trappers sold her to a farm for ten dollars a foot or if she's in some Florida cypress pond under a rickety wooden bridge, where Yankee tourists pay a dollar to watch her sleep. Could be somebody's sitting on a South Georgia alligator wallet right now, or carrying a South Georgia alligator handbag, or wearing a pair of South Georgia alligator shoes. But that old proverb about walking a mile in another man's moccasins takes on a certain irony there.

To tell the truth, people don't seem to have much sympathy for the alligator. It's kind of an ugly duckling, and the fact that it eats whatever live bodies happen to enter the water doesn't endear it to the guardians of children and little gray dogs. But despite a reputation for menace, the alligator can have a singular kind of appeal— can have a power, and a mystery, and a magical kind of charm as she glides around a pond on a summer night, piercing the darkness with her jack-o'-lantern eyes, looking for her supper.

panther tracks

"You ort to carry a gun when you go back in them woods," Gene was telling me as he pounded his tractor with a hammer.

"I've been walking back there for nearly five years and never had a problem," I argued, leaning against the tree by the barn and chewing on a sour weed. This was a conversation we'd had often.

"It don't take but once," he said, lifting an eyebrow at me.

"Animals aren't going to attack unless they feel threatened, Gene," I said. "Anyway, the dogs'll scare them off."

"That panther'll eat them dogs."

I took the sour weed out of my mouth and looked at him. "What panther?"

He glanced at me, then turned and disappeared into the barn.

"What panther?" I yelled.

He came back holding a wrench and bent down again to the tractor. "They's wild dogs, they's rattlers—" He fumbled with a screw. "You never know what you might run up on back there in them woods."

"Come on, Gene. There aren't any panthers in Georgia," I said authoritatively, coming around where I could see his face.

"They's a panther 'round here, all right." He looked up at me. "Ain't you seen it yet?"

"Oh pooh, Gene."

"Me and Alice heard it."

"Where?"

"Down there by your place. Right before you moved in."

"What did it sound like?"

"Sounded like a woman hollerin'."

"It was probably just a screech owl."

"It was a panther."

"How do you know?"

"I was born knowing. That's why I'm tellin' you. You ort to carry a gun when you go back yonder."

"Hmph," I said, and changed the subject.

After that day, three years passed and I didn't hear another word about a panther. At first, I did listen at night for panther sounds, but I never heard anything except, once, a screech owl on the other side of the pond, and that was bad enough.

*S*creech owls are small birds about the size of a pinecone. They have round yellow eyes and prominent ears and a tremulous, descending wail that sounds, in Gene's words, like a woman hollering.

Screech owls are furious little birds, and in defense of their nests they're fearless. If you happen by a screech owl nest at night, the owl will fly right down and hit you on the head. So I wasn't about to go looking for the one that was sitting in a pine tree across the pond at two o'clock in the morning, keeping the dogs and me awake.

I was standing at the screen door of the cabin in the pale darkness of the clear moonlit night, watching Queenie pace the yard. Max was sitting by the bank of the pond with his ears pricked up. I was thinking about the two remedies for screech owls that Gene had given me.

"If you take your hands outen your pockets, that'll shut 'em up," he had told me one night after supper, sitting in the easy chair in his den.

"That's absurd, Gene."

"It'd work, though."

"You mean if I put my hands in my pockets and then take them back out again?"

"Yep. If you lay a broomstick across the door, that'd work, too."

"But, Gene. That doesn't make any sense."

"It don't have to make sense, long as it works."

I shook my head at him and went home.

Now I took the big flashlight down from its hook by the door and went out the screen door and stood on the back steps. Maybe if I shine the flashlight at him, he'll hush, I thought. I cast the light over the pond and into the woods. It didn't work.

"Shut up, owl!" I yelled. But that just made Queenie bark.

Around three, I went in and got the broom out of the corner by the refrigerator. I wasn't about to try standing in the door and taking my hands out of my pockets. That just seemed too ridiculous. But I did lay the broom across the open doorway, and the owl hushed. I've never heard a screech owl out here since.

*L*ast year when November was half over I was walking along the edge of the Dills' field of harvested cotton, looking for arrowheads, when a movement caused me to look up. Fifty paces ahead of me a dark, long-bodied feline shape emerged out of the trees on my right and glided across my path. The instant I realized that the shape wasn't one of the dogs I stopped dead still, wondering where Max and Queenie were and trying to feel which way the wind was blowing.

Suddenly the shape paused and turned its head toward me. The face was small, triangular, and paler, I thought, than the long legs and narrow trunk. Then I saw the dogs ahead, coming out of the stand of pines on my right. But they were moving away. They hadn't seen the animal.

After a moment, it went on. I watched it until it disappeared into the trees half a mile away, its movement through the field startling flocks of sparrows into the air. I searched for tracks for an hour but never found them, having been so startled to see a wild panther in a cotton field that I hadn't the presence of mind to notice landmarks and didn't know where to look.

At least I thought it was a panther, although I couldn't be sure. I'd heard legends about panthers in South Georgia when I was a child, how they stole babies out of their cribs and carried them off into the woods, raided the chicken coops, killed the calves. But just as I'd never seen an alligator that wasn't on television, I'd never seen a panther except in a book. So no matter what Gene said, I wasn't convinced that panthers existed in the South except as bobcats nurtured into legendary proportions by a lively cultural imagination.

Nevertheless, when I got home I called Gene and asked him what a panther looked like. It turned out that I was the fourth person to see it. One of the Dills' boys on a three-wheeler in the woods had rounded a bend near the alligator pond and found it standing in the road. The Dills' ninety-pound bulldog crawled trembling into the boy's lap and refused to move. The boy wheeled around and raced back to the house. Now he won't go three-wheeling in the woods any more. Others had seen the panther near our pond and crossing the paved road over the creek.

Since then, Gene has told me about monkeys spotted in abandoned barns, hyenas in the fields, black bears by the creek, and cougars shot and killed in Willacoochee. For a long time, I would have thought it was all nonsense. Now I'm not so sure. Having captured the subtle alligator, sighted the legendary panther with my own eyes, and spooked a screech owl with a broomstick, I can't say any more which things are real—and which are just stories.

different light

One early morning in May I was driving to my paying job as a public relations writer for a college in a town thirty miles away from my cabin. I was off in that nether land where people go when they drive, thinking about all I needed to do. Thinking about lost loves. Thinking about Max always digging out from under the fence and visiting Gene's house across the road, defying the big trucks that hurl themselves down this remote stretch of blacktop, making up time.

But then I noticed, after I crossed the bridge over the river, something different there. Something about the light. It seemed harsher somehow, brighter, the outline of shadows sharper than I remembered over that piece of road I'd traveled nearly half my life.

The change was something I sensed, rather than saw, like the way I'd have felt coming home after a long walk and thinking, when I opened the cabin door, that the sofa seemed a few inches closer to the chair than I remembered and that my book, which I thought I'd left open on the chair, was now on the table, beside the lamp.

So as I drove down that altered length of road I glanced to the left, not knowing what I was looking for, really—and I saw why the light had changed. And I slowed the car to a crawl because I was experiencing that sinking feeling that sounds so clichéd but is exactly, it turns out, the way you feel when your breathing is shocked into a halt, when your heart feels pressed and aches in your chest like a child who's been slapped and doesn't understand why.

The forest was gone. The forest was gone and re-placed by nothing, except a logging truck and a caution sign and some of those orange plastic cones that divide the cars going by at seventy from the small, slow people who resurface the highways in the city. I could see the river from the road, where it wove around a forest floor I had never seen.

The earth was shoved down to level, littered with splinters and the naked stumps of sweet gum, water oak, maple, and pine, and heaps of leaf-covered branches exposed in the sun, torn from the trees as they had fallen. An indigo snake lay dead in the ditch. A man stood leaning against a gray pickup, smoking a cigarette, waiting for the rest of his crew. He watched me with an air of smug indif-ference as I watched him, my astonishment, I'm certain, plain on my face.

As I drove away, to my job in town, I begrudged the sense of helplessness I felt. I begrudged the shift of light out of softness, out of the rich darkness of forest, out of green. I begrudged the loss of nesting places for blue herons and barred owls and gray squirrels, the dens of gopher turtles, foxes, coyotes, and indigo snakes. I wanted to turn the car around, fly to that man who leaned so candidly against his pickup, plead with him to put it all back the way it was, the way I remembered it. I wanted to drive that road again not knowing those changes.

For as long as I can remember, MaRe and I were the best of friends. Many of our days together we spent out here at this cabin by the pond, cleaning, planting, fishing, talking, laughing. Years after I was grown, through all my uprootings and turnings and heartbreaks, she remained the clearest, the truest, the most certain vision of my life. I wrapped her around me like a blanket and survived. Then I moved back down to Georgia and came to live on this land, and she died.

Change rides hard on the soft back of certainty. Change moves in ways and moments you least expect, tearing down the trees that filter out the harsher light that you're afraid will blind you, leaving the life you've bound yourself up in lying in splinters at your feet. You can't turn around. You can't put things back and you don't want to drive that stretch of altered road home.

But somehow, because the change forces you to do it, you do drive down that road, and you learn to know the new light. You watch its tones and shadows, and you get on. I know this different light, now. I know the way it moves.

And I understand, too, that one day, someone who loves rivers will come to that wide space of forest floor that I drove by in dismay, and be glad for the way the sunlight glides across the water free from leaf and branch, and warms the open banks, and draws the shadows out long and clear over the road.

the generosity of strangers

The gas needle was dead on "E" at seven o'clock on a cold Friday morning and I was already thirty minutes from the cabin—too far to turn around—and thirty minutes from Valdosta, where I planned to end up. But Lakeland was only five miles down the road, and I had a few dollar bills in my wallet. In my car, two dollars' worth of gas can get me all the way to Macon. So I didn't think much about what could happen to a small woman stranded on an unfamiliar backcountry road alone until I headed into Lakeland and reached for my pocketbook and realized I'd left my wallet at home.

I looked around for change. Nothing. Not even a

dime under the seat. And no quarter to call Gene for help. I thought about risking the drive to Valdosta, but decided it would be foolish. I thought about begging a gallon of gas from the station attendant and promising to come back later and pay for it, but I couldn't imagine anybody believing I'd really come back.

In fact, I didn't know a soul in Lakeland to ask for a short-term loan, and besides, I had no identification to show that I was anybody. My license, my credit cards, every piece of evidence that might prove to a stranger that I was who I said I was, all of it was secreted in the various folds and zippered pockets of my green leather wallet, which was lying on the table at the cabin beside the milk glass from breakfast.

The only plan I could come up with was to go to the police with my story and beg a dollar for gas. I pulled into the lot by the station, yanked up the parking brake, took a deep breath, and got out. Two officers standing at the entrance to the building eyed me as I walked toward them with a tentative smile. I imagined their bodies tensing under their uniforms. I spilled my story as soon as I reached them.

"All I need is a dollar," I told them. "I didn't know where else to go."

They asked me questions. They wanted to know the facts, wanted me to say again where I was going, why, what time I'd left home, things like that. Checking out my story, I thought, and I was hoping they wouldn't ask for the license I didn't have with me. But eventually they started chuckling, and after a minute, one of them reached into his pocket and handed me two crumpled dollar bills.

"Oh, this is too much," I said, offering one of the bills back. "Really. All I need is a dollar."

"Naw. Keep it. You might need to make a phone call."

Then the other officer held out four dollars. "Here's a little more," he said.

"Really," I said, "that's so nice of you but I don't need all that. I can get money in Valdosta."

"Oh, go on," he said, grinning. "Take it. You gotta eat lunch."

"No, I, really—" I started to say, and then I got it. These men *wanted* me to have their money. They wanted to buy my gas, and they wanted to buy me lunch. They wanted to rescue me.

And to tell the truth, that was okay with me. I didn't mind being rescued. It felt good. So I took their six dollars and thanked them kindly and went on my way. For lunch I bought a cheeseburger and some french fries at the Dairy Queen, and with my chocolate malt I toasted the public servants of Lakeland, Georgia, and I've felt grateful and warm about that day ever since.

s o l d

Death is the mother of beauty.

WALLACE STEVENS

It was a Thursday afternoon, one of those mild days near the end of November when the weather comes in warm and breezy after a week of near-freezing nights and cold, overcast days. I went outside dressed for a walk and found myself too hot even in the shadows, had to change from long sleeves and jeans into shorts and a T-shirt.

I was in a peaceful mood. Nearing the end of a stressful few months, anxious to get on to the next thing, now I stood on the back steps, listening to the birds, trying to think of the right word to describe the sound of the wind in the pines. Soughing. The wind was soughing, soft, barely brushing the leaves of the taller hardwoods. The pond was a clear gray-green that shone back in muted shades the reds and golds, oranges and yellows of the gums and maples on the banks.

I opened the back gate and walked down the path to the dam, following the dogs, who were frisky and ran in front of me. The colors of the day were deep and rich, the sky that winter shade of clean, sparkling blue, the air sweet-smelling with a hint of pine—and the pictures that sur-rounded me seemed so undemanding and pure that when I reached the spot halfway across the dam where I always stop to look back across the water at this red tarpaper and rusted tin roof of a cabin, I found myself grieving. I could see the light filtering golden through a red maple, just beyond where the boat leans against the pine tree by MaRe's blueberry bushes. A turtle plopped into the water off a fallen branch, and a little blue heron left his perch on the drain and flew into the woods behind me, and I could not reconcile those images with the picture in my mind of myself closing that red gate at the end of the drive for the last time and heading down the road northward and away, knowing I could never come back. Even though the farm was not yet sold, even though I knew I would have to leave it anyway, at least for a while, the idea of parting from it for good was a weight that bore down so hard on the back of my neck that when I finally went on to continue my walk I found it hard to lift my head. I didn't want to see.

I walked up the hill through a clearing between two stands of young pine trees, the space covered with wild blackberry vines, goldenrod and blue-eyed grasses still blooming, and pale purple gerardia gone to seed. The cold nights had beaten down the undergrowth so I could finally get through it without tripping over the low, tangled vines or scratching my legs on their thorns. The end of the path opened into a cotton field divided into two long stretches by Donnie's airstrip. Still unharvested, the cotton remained as soft white clumps on the brown, drying stems, some with pink blossoms just opened. The grass on the airstrip had turned to a dusty gold. To the west and south were planted pines; to the east, a strip of hardwood, wild plum, huckleberry, mimosa, and chinaberry and then a dirt path through more cotton.

At the far end of the airstrip, half a mile away across the paved road, a century-old red tobacco barn had at last begun to lean. I liked to stand at the end of the airstrip and look back at that barn, pretending that no paved road ran there, that the landscape was as undisturbed as it had been when my great-grandfather was alive.

When I reached the Dills' wider cotton fields farther on, the dogs disappeared into the pine trees and left me alone. I walked for a while, trying to calm my feelings, when suddenly a half-grown armadillo appeared on the path a few paces in front of me. The dogs had already spotted it, and they were on top of it in seconds, tormenting it, driving it back toward the woods. I was torn by the armadillo's confusion, yet I was unwilling to interfere with the dogs to save it. The armadillo was wild and, as horrible as the killing was to witness, and as cruel as it seemed, I had come to accept the process as natural.

Even as I watched, Queenie clamped her jaws down on the animal's back and crushed its tough armor. As her teeth sank through to skin, I could hear the armadillo's weak squeals. I walked away, into the field, but I couldn't escape the sound of Queenie ripping at the armadillo's hide, piercing its throat, tearing into its internal organs.

$\mathcal{S}$ince that day, the farm has been sold. I had not the resources to buy it, and my own small protests were ineffectual against the inexorable coming to pass of a circumstance that I had no power to change and a process that I had no influence to stop. This afternoon, when I went walking, I found fluorescent pink plastic tape tied to sticks, wrapped around tree trunks, stuck onto metal spikes in the ground, marking off the property lines. Until today I had never known the shape of this land.

But shapes, definitions, boundaries, they have no place here. One drafty cabin, several ponds, a half-dozen fields, and thousands of trees with their scattered trails— none of these have I ever owned except in the way they move in me through the spirits of my ancestors. As the armadillo taught me so eloquently, the part of me that anguishes is the part of me that is caught, the part of me that longs to remain wrapped around the feel of *this* earth between my fingers and the smell of *these* bream beds in May and the taste of *these* blueberries on my tongue and the sound of *these* whippoorwills at dusk and the memories of all the lifelong associations they hold for me. Until the day comes when I can let them go, I rely on the chance to know new earth and the generosity of an aunt and uncle who are no longer strangers.

$\mathcal{A}$fter my parents divorced, I lost touch with my dad's side of the family. But I was always fond of his sister,

Helen, and last fall, I called her. When I mentioned that I would be leaving the pond, they asked me where I would go. I told them I hadn't decided. They offered me their mountain cabin in North Georgia to live in.

"It's rustic," said Aunt Helen, "but I guess you're used to that."

"Does it have hot water?"

"Oh, yes."

"That's not rustic. Can you drink the water, too?"

"Oh, yes. The well's thirty feet deep."

Besides that, Aunt Helen said, the cabin is well built, so it stays warm in winter.

Wow, I thought. Drinkable well water. Hot water from a tap. Warm winter nights. So much for the hard life. I'm climbing into the lap of luxury. The only thing left to want is a bathtub.

So the dogs and I, we'll soon be giving over the ways of pond, pine, turtle, and armadillo to learn the ways of mountain—and scarlet oak, wild holly, trout stream, and ice storm. I've got six months yet but I'm already packing, trying to scale down to the essential. The cabin up north is only half the size of this one, including the screened porch on warm days. But there's hot water. From a tap. The idea bewilders me. Never mind slow time. It's the simplicity I'm after.

There's no pond where we're going and I'll have no back step, but there is a clear creek down the mountainside and from the cabin's north window I can see the Appalachian Trail across the valley, where it runs along the top of Black Mountain. In those regions above the fall line, the light has a different texture. Its edges are sharp and the air is clear. The oak leaves shimmer in that clarity, like Colorado aspens golden in autumn. In winter, it snows.

I don't know the birds there. I don't know the rise and fall of the land, or the way the wind sounds after midnight, or the color of the sky after a rain. But I will watch and I will write, and the pictures will tell me tales.

I was walking with my dogs at the edge of Gene's cornfield one day when a ragged coyote darted out from under some chinaberry trees and cut across the track in front of me. He threw me a frank look on the way by and I never saw him again after that. I did see one of his relatives, though: a coyote pup, shot in the head with a rifle. He was lying under a water oak by a logging trail a mile or so from the cabin.

I see a lot of dead animals out here in the country, especially during hunting season. It's surprising, in fact, how many different kinds of animals get killed when deer season comes in—coons, rabbits, beavers, squirrels, coyotes, foxes, armadillos, possums, crows, owls, and on and on. Sometimes I think all it has to do is be moving and—I don't take too many afternoon walks in the woods during deer season.

But I see a good many live animals, too. One morning, I saw Queenie holding something furry in her mouth. The first time I saw her holding something like that, it had a long skinny tail attached to it, which stuck out through a gap in her teeth. When she saw me looking, she crunched down, chewed twice, and swallowed. After that I noticed a steady decline in my mouse population.

But this time Queenie's captive had no tail and, to my

surprise, when I reached for it, instead of crunching down, she opened her mouth, and out hopped a baby duck— about the size of a mouse but its feet were a lot bigger. I didn't know whether its mother would take it back or not, and it was small enough to make a mouthful for a snapping turtle, but I took it to the other end of the pond anyway and let it go and that little duck took out over the water like a speedboat. That was last summer. Now, where I used to have one duck, I have two.

I had a beaver at the pond one summer, too. It chewed down the trees at night. In the afternoons, it swam, while Max sat straight up at the edge of the water with that one ear flopped over like a windless flag. The beaver would look at Max, swim up close, then dive under and pop up at the other end of the pond. The beaver wasn't around for long, though, because when it went over to the Harpers' pond for a change of scenery it got caught in a trap.

I have an old friend, a logger, who has worked these woods for years, and he tells me that life loves the destruction of southern forests. When the trees come down, he says, wildflowers that have lain dormant in the overhanging darkness for years suddenly open out into the sunlight. Grasses and undergrowth flourish and make food and cover abundant and easy for deer and indigo snakes to find. In fifteen years, he says, pines and water oaks and sweet gums grow back as tall as they were before. It's an essentially stable universe—as Loren Eiseley put it—and this is the guarantee that makes life possible. It's the immutable law of physics: for every action there exists an equal and opposite reaction. So Queenie can swallow a mouse, or the Harpers can trap a beaver; I end up with two ducks and let the rattlesnake go. Last week I saw a new beaver in the pond.

The harder I clutch at the things I love, the harder life works to wrench me free. So I'll close the red gate behind me and head northward on the breath of summer. There's a rare beauty in those mountains, I'm told, and stories for the trails to tell, and the land has a wide character.

gene

$\mathcal{T}$he January day I told Gene I would be moving away when summer came, I found him under the pole barn he put up two years ago. He was welding together the parts of an airplane he plans to finish building by the time he retires from farming. This year, Gene is sixty-six.

South Georgia experienced a bad drought last growing season, and while I explained to him where I'd be living, the heavy equipment behind him was noisily clear-cutting the seven acres of timber that surrounded his brick house on the hill, so he could pay his bills.

Gene has been farming Pop's land since he was nine-teen. "Mr. Willis didn't know the first thing about farming," he told me once, reminiscing about their long relationship. "He'd come out here and tell me how to put things and I'd put 'em that way. Then after he left I'd put 'em back right. But he was always out here. All the time. Helping."

On the living Gene and Alice have earned from farming they've raised three children here, lost a son to illness here, brought up grandsons here. At one time or another they've had horses, motorcycles, antique cars, cats, dogs, cows, and airplanes. "It's not many families that's been able to stay on a farm as long as we have," Gene says.

Of course, long ago Gene and Alice bought the property they live on, and Pop's fields aren't the only ones he leases any more, so the sale of our farm won't mean they'll have to move. Still, even though he doesn't say much about it, I'm sure the parceling out of this land has been as hard on him as anybody.

Now I was sitting on a stool, watching him drill holes in the wing of his airplane. "I'm writing about you in my book," I told him. "Don't sue me."

"Amy, Amy, Amy," he said, shaking his head. "You tellin' them lies again?"

"It's all a lie."

He grunted. "Tell you what. You can write about me if you promise to let me fly you in this here airplane when I get it finished."

"Ha. I'll be too far away by then."

"Naw, sir. This here plane'll go six hundred miles. I'll come get you." He grinned and handed me the box some of the airplane parts had come in.

It was true. Six hundred miles at a stretch. The plane

was a Kitfox single-engine two-seater. They go a hundred and ten miles an hour. "Everything in one complete box," said the box. "No special skills needed."

"They've made over twenty-five hunnerd of these here airplanes by now," Gene said. "Mine's number eighteen hunnerd and five."

"My Lord," I said, reading the box.

"What?"

" 'No special skills needed.' This is right up your alley, Gene."

"Hmph."

"What color is it?"

"I'll have to paint it. I was thinking yaller with a blue stripe. Or maybe blue with a yaller stripe." He drilled a few more holes. "Yaller and blue, anyway."

"Will Alice ride in it?"

"I reckon she will. She's been up with Donnie once."

I patted one of Gene's five dogs on the head.

"When you leave out of here next summer, I reckon there'll be some crying then, won't there," said Gene.

Whether he meant me, or himself, I didn't know. I looked away. "I don't think about it."

"No, I don't reckon you do."

"You know, I appreciate all you've done for me, Gene," I said in a burst of emotion.

"Yep. And you owe me a pile of money, too."

When I got Max, Gene built him a doghouse. When I got Queenie, Gene put up a dog pen behind the cabin. While MaRe was alive, he built a handrail for her by the steps. Two weeks ago he cut down the diseased pine tree that was threatening to break off in the middle and fall on my bed.

"Good grief, Gene," I told him when I saw the trunk. "You could have cut it down below two feet."

"I wanted to leave you a stump to set on and fish."

"I can't sit on a pine stump, Gene. I'd stick to the sap."

"I reckon you'd better not set there, then," he said.

Last summer, Gene spent all afternoon helping me build a new back gate and then he hung it for me. He keeps the trail over the dam mowed so I can walk it, he has repaired my leaky faucet twice, and he once picked a fried earwig out of the electrical contact on the water pump. One night around midnight a girlfriend and I were watching a movie when I heard a volley of shotgun blasts nearby. I called Gene's house. Alice answered.

"I think I've got hunters," I said. "Do y'all hear that?"

"Oh, that's Gene," said Alice. "He's out in the yard, shooting at armadillos. We wondered if you could hear it."

"My word. How many armadillos has he got out there, Alice? It sounds like a war."

"Oh, just one," she said, laughing. "Gene just can't hit it. He's not a very good shot."

Speaking of shooting, I moved into the cabin at the beginning of hunting season, and for the first few months, until I was better able to tell where the gunshots were coming from, Gene often climbed the front gate and came racing down to the cabin in the middle of the night. I'd call him because I needed him to scare off the hunters I thought I heard prowling around in the woods on the other side of the pond. We never found any hunters in the woods, though, so after a while I stopped calling Gene after midnight.

Gene may not be a crack shot when it comes to armadillos, but he can wield one heck of an axe. I once saw him chop the head clean off a dead raccoon with a single stroke. My dogs had killed it at the pond, and I'd been instructed to send the head to the diagnostic lab for analysis because we were having a rabies epidemic. I knew I didn't have the strength to do the job myself, so Gene and I took the raccoon way out in the woods and Gene cut the animal's head off. Then we burned the body and did an Indian dance around the funeral pyre.

Sometimes Gene comes over and climbs up on the roof to hammer two-by-fours into the holes around the eaves, to keep the squirrels out of the attic. It doesn't really work, but we like to do it anyway. One day I asked Gene why there are so many holes covered with hail screen on the east outside wall of the cabin. He told me that was where Pop had shot at squirrels. "He was drunk," Gene said.

"Was he shooting from the inside or the outside?"

"From the inside *to* the outside. He had clumb up a ladder in the cabin and had his whole head and shoulders in the crawl space, shooting at the squirrels. They was always bad to get in there."

"Did he get any?"

"Not as I remember," said Gene, slamming another two-by-four under the eave.

Gene has come to my rescue with engine oil, coolant, air for my tires, superglue for my rearview mirror, and other sundry automotive necessities. I drove over to his barn this afternoon on the way to the grocery store because I thought my tires were too low. He ambled out the back door of his house when he saw me coming. "What you need?" he said.

"I think my tires are low."

"That's high," he said.

"How much?"

"Oh, 'bout five or ten dollars a pound."

"Ha. You can add it to my bill."

"Uh-huh. That's getting right on up there." He got the air hose out of the barn and walked around my car looking at the tires.

I pointed at the left front. "Don't you think that looks low?"

"Yep." He squatted down and put his hand on the tire.

"Maybe it has a leak," I said.

"It must do." He looked at me. "Or maybe not."

"Well, that's profound," I said.

"Uh-huh."

He put air in the tires, and then he nodded to his truck. "You're gonna have to buy me some new wheels pretty soon," he said.

"How come?"

"Max done rusted all mine out."

"Huh? Oh. Good grief, Gene."

"He stays up here all the time."

"I know it. It's because of Nellie," I said. Nellie was one of Gene's dogs.

"I don't think he likes it down at your place," he said.

Gene put the air hose back in the barn and came and leaned against the disc that was attached to one of his tractors. I was sitting on the hood of my car.

"You probably don't have to spend too much on groceries, do you," said Gene.

"Why?"

"You probably don't eat too much."

"Well, today I'm out of everything. I'm even out of toilet paper."

"That's bad."

"Yeah."

"Ain't you got a old Sears catalogue?"

"You can't buy groceries out of a Sears catalogue, Gene."

"No. But you can use it for toilet paper."

"Gene!" I said, and I climbed down and got in the car. "Hold on to Max so he doesn't chase me," I said as I started the engine.

"He ain't going nowhere," said Gene, but he bent down and grabbed Max's collar anyway.

If Gene has done his share to keep my life at a level of relative comfort, so has Alice. She has cooked ladyfinger peas with fatback for me in summer and made little individual ground beef casseroles for me when I was sick. She's dug fresh turnips for me out of her garden, fed my cats and cleaned out their litter box when I was gone, loaned me Coca-Colas and eggs and cornmeal and dog food, and shown me how to make self-rising buttermilk biscuits. We've spent long hours in intricate discussions about life, death, God, farming, dreams, and the nature of the universe.

Alice married Gene when she was sixteen and I most admire her for sticking with him. The two of them grew up poor and spent the first third of their lives poor. Now they, too, live in relative comfort, but maintaining is always a struggle.

"Let me see," Gene said, starting a new set of holes in his Kitfox airplane wing. "At forty dollars a hour, I reckon you owe me about several thousand dollars by now. I don't know how much you owe Alice."

"Ha. I'll send you the royalties from the book sales."

"Well, Amy, you got to be smart at something, I reckon."

I left him then, bent over the directions for building his plane. As I walked away, I heard him call out to me.

"If you need any help with your book, now, you call me," he said. "Remember I graduated. Made it all the way through the seventh grade."

I waved and nodded and smiled. Apparently, I thought as I headed for the cabin, that's how many grades it takes to make you real.

queenie

Queenie died on a warm night at the end of February. I had come in late, and Max was strangely quiet when he met me at the car. He didn't wag his tail, didn't jump up and put his paws in my lap, just stood beside the open door, looking at me.

Queenie had been getting out of the yard, I knew, going around the end of the fence where it no longer met the water: the level of the pond had dropped several feet since last summer's drought. Since she'd discovered the way out, she'd begun traveling with Max. But where Max was always street-smart, Queenie was heedless of the cars and trucks that came whipping down these paved country roads. That February night, the instant I saw that she wasn't at the gate to meet me, I knew she was dead. I knew it before I saw the light blinking on my answering machine, just as I knew the call was from Gene. His voice played back to me on the recorder even as I was on the phone to him, asking what had happened.

Gene had found Queenie beside the road soon after I'd left home and put her in the back of his pickup. He'd bring her over, he said, and help me bury her.

The front gate is padlocked, so I had to walk up the path and unlock it to let Gene drive in, and I could see him through the trees. He was standing in front of the truck, waiting for me. I saw him dash tears from his face with the back of his hand as I came around the corner with Max.

I opened the gate and went to Gene's truck and climbed into the bed of the pickup, where he had laid Queenie on a sheet of cardboard. Except for the small amount of blood that had leaked from her mouth, there was no evidence of her wounds.

"What happened to her, Gene?"

"Just hit real hard. Stopped her heart," he said, coming around the back of the truck. "Look at her legs, Amy. She didn't kick or nothing."

"What does that mean?"

"I don't think she suffered none."

Queenie's thick fur was silvery in the glare of light from the truck cab, and her large brown eyes held a distant look. A deer had been hit near where Gene had found her, he said—she and Max had probably gone to investigate the deer. I stroked her face, thinking, Well, it's finally happened, what I've been trying to avoid all these years. None of my dogs had ever died in my care. As I'd moved from place to place, I'd given them all away.

I took a breath and climbed back down.

"What can I say, Gene. Not that I didn't expect it, sooner or later."

"I hate it to happen to Queenie, though."

I climbed into the cab with Max, and Gene drove us back to the pond.

It took us a while to decide where to bury her. Queenie was a big dog, and we needed a place where the tree roots wouldn't be too thick and the dirt would be soft enough to dig deep. We started a hole near where I'd buried the cats, on the west side of the cabin near the fence. The moon was only a quarter full, and even though the night was clear there wasn't enough light to see by, so Gene trained his truck lights on the spot where we were digging. Max lay nearby and watched.

It took us a long time to get down even a few inches. The ground was hard and the tree roots were tough as old tire rubber, so it was a backbreaking business. And every time I put my shovel down, I heard a buzzing sound.

"You hear that?" I asked Gene.

"Might be yellow jackets," he said. He shone his flashlight into the hole, and I turned over some dirt and pine straw, but we didn't see any yellow jackets.

We kept digging. We got down another six inches.

"Sounds like people talking," I said. "Like they're a long way off."

"Maybe you got hunters."

"In February?"

"Not likely."

Then Gene pushed his shovel under a maple root and we heard a crunching sound and he came up with a load of white gravel. "Uh-oh," he said, shaking his head.

"What is that?"

"We done dug into the sewer line, Amy."

"Oh, no."

"Yep. We got to cover this back up. I smell it, now."

"Did we break it?"

"No. But we can't put Queenie here."

"Was that what was buzzing? The sewer line?"

"Uh-huh."

"Damn."

"Better cover it back up."

We covered it back up.

We walked around the yard and decided to move to the other side, near the east gate, under a dogwood tree near the water. I went in and got a bottle of wine out of the refrigerator, gulped some down, and brought the bottle back with me. Max lay down by a pine tree and watched. As soon as I started digging, the buzzing started again.

"You hear that?" I asked Gene.

"Sure do, Amy."

"I guess it wasn't the sewer line, then."

"I reckon not."

We dug a few minutes more, and the buzzing kept on.

"Is it some kind of frog?" I said.

"None I ever heard." Suddenly Gene stopped digging and looked at my shovel. "Oh," he said.

"What?"

"You got bumblebees."

"Where?" I dropped the shovel and jumped back.

In the handle of my shovel was a perfectly round hole, about a quarter-inch in diameter, where bumblebees had bored into the wood. Now they were inside the handle, where they had crept in as they had hollowed it out. Every time I jarred the shovel, they buzzed.

Gene plugged the hole with a piece of green branch off the dogwood tree, but he told me to remind him to unplug it again when we got through. "Them bees pollinate my crops," he said. "I wouldn't have nothing without them bees."

After an hour we were several feet down. Gene was standing in the hole, breaking up roots and taking out heaping shovelfuls of dirt. I was watching from above, unable to get my shovel in around him. To tell the truth, all night long he'd done most of the work while I'd just fumbled around the edges.

"Why don't you get out and let me dig some," I said, worried about him twisting the knee he'd been complaining of.

"I ort to tell you," he said. "Gravediggers gets more than forty dollars a hour."

"You can have some wine." I offered him the bottle.

"I don't believe so. Wine don't set well with me."

"Get out of there and let me do some of the work."

"I believe I will come out and blow awhile. Just to get my breath." He stepped up to climb out, but he lost his footing.

"Don't fall, Gene."

"If I fall I'll sue you."

He came out and stood beside the hole and leaned on his shovel, and I got in and started to dig.

"I believe you'd get more done if you had a teaspoon, Amy," he said.

Presently, I saw him look up at the sky. "We might not have enough dirt to fill the hole up, depending on the moon," he said.

I stopped and looked at him. "What moon?"

"If the moon is full you have too much dirt. You can make a mound."

"I don't get it, Gene. Whatever you take out of the hole, you just put back in."

"I done dug enough holes to know." He paused. "I wish we had enough to make a mound for Queenie."

"The moon is waxing. It's about a quarter full."

"We ain't going to have enough," he said, shaking his head.

After a long time, we finished digging, and we laid Queenie down in the grave and filled it back up. Gene was right. There was barely enough dirt to cover the hole, and not enough for a mound. Afterward, we stood for a few minutes, and then Gene took the dogwood plug out of the handle of my shovel, wished me sweet dreams, and went home.

The next morning, a woman I know who has a childlike naiveté about proprieties saw me crying by the coffee machine. She asked me what had happened and I told her. "Oh, is that all," she said, chuckling. "I thought it was something really serious!" She patted my shoulder as she pushed past me and went back to her desk.

A friend standing nearby gave me a puzzled look. "Good grief," he said. "That just about sums up all of life, doesn't it."

*M*ax was bewildered for a long time after Queenie died. He would lie in the yard for hours, looking toward the gate, on the spot where she used to watch for him when he was gone. He was lethargic and unresponsive, and he wouldn't bark, and he wouldn't run after his ball. Even when the otter and the beavers swam in the pond, he wouldn't make a sound—only sat on the bank and watched. One day I saw him race around the corner of the cabin, only to stop suddenly and stare at Queenie's dog house, then turn around and trot back to his place by the gate.

As for me, until it rained I could still see Queenie's paw prints in the fields, and some days, when I went walking, I imagined she would come back home, bounding out of the woods to meet me. A few days after she died, I found a tuft of her fur near the back steps, where she used to sit with her head in my lap.

But most of all it was Queenie's largeness that I missed, her ninety pounds of muscle rounded into softness by black and silver fur long enough to hide my fingers in. Her largeness made everything about her vigorous and noisy, and her dying left wide spaces in the yard vacant and quiet when she was no longer there to fill them.

Nevertheless, Max and I, we're getting on. Little by little, Max has been shaking the blues. I've seen him chasing dragonflies, and today he's been standing on the bank of the pond, barking at the minnows.

Me, I sit on the back steps with my coffee and notice that the grass is growing back over Queenie's grave under the dogwood tree, near the water. And that Gene's crops are in the ground now. And that in the handle of my shovel, there are bumblebees.

time folds

Sometimes I sit out in the yard in one of those yellow lawn chairs with the frayed bottoms and watch the light move on the pond. I like to think out there. One afternoon in late March turned out warm and windy, so I went outside to sit in the chair and I thought I'd take some notes, work out some things to write about. I didn't have long. I had to be somewhere at seven.

The dogwoods were beginning to bloom and from my chair I could see a half-dozen white blossoms on the pond side of the southernmost tree. This hollow is shaded and cool, so its dogwoods are some of the last to bloom. I'll write about those dogwoods, I thought, how they bloom late every year.

But I heard a red-winged blackbird singing, and the sound put me in mind of how warm the winter had been, and how it seemed early yet for blackbirds, and I thought of Pop. He was a rough, reckless, drinking man, but he knew the subtleties of fishing, and he taught them to me.

On summer afternoons when I was six and loved the outdoors, Roy Rogers, and dogs more than anything else in the world, Pop often came to the tiny brown house where my family lived near town and took me in his light-green Buick down the long, curving miles of country road to this pond. He'd take his tackle box and rods and reels out of the trunk, and I'd grab the cricket cage and the box of earthworms off the seat, and we'd load ourselves into the beaten johnboat with welded-over holes and a concrete block for an anchor.

Pop taught me to put my whole hand down into the cricket cage. To hold a cricket by its back. To push the hook through its tough white underside. To hook an earthworm three times through. He taught me to know the dark, close smell of bream beds, to seek out those light patches of sand in the shallows and near the banks. He taught me where the bass held themselves cool and still under the low overhanging branches of the water oaks and red maples. He taught me to cast into the shadows. To draw my line in easy. To know the snap of a largemouth bass from the nip of a bream. To wait. Into those moments, into all those quiet, careful moments of my learning, came the song of the red-winged blackbird, touching me, moving me, even at six, out of the boat where I sat watching my line play across the water, into the whole greater song of wood and field that surrounded me.

But sometimes into the silence Pop's rough voice broke like a sudden violent undertow, wrenching me back, folding me into my solitary self. I moved around too much, he said. I made too much noise. I got my line tangled. I scared the fish away.

So I learned to whisper my questions, to move softly in a boat, to pull my paddle silent through the water and lift it out again without knocking the gunwales, so that the only sound was the sound of boat gliding over pond, the dip of anchor, the waves lapping, lapping, lapping as we sat, casting our lines and reeling them in, casting lines and reeling in.

When I was a teenager, I sang in a church choir. Not long ago, the choir had a reunion. Most of us had been living in other parts of the country, hadn't seen each other in the more than two decades we'd been apart. It didn't matter. Somehow, at forty, we knew each other instantly, in old, familiar ways. For a weekend, we remembered. Re-experienced. Lived completely as we'd lived before, in all the open, honest, tingling intimacy of adolescents out past midnight. "You pick up where you left off," said my logger friend who is also musical, as a handful of us sat marveling over how we felt, drinking beer, breaking curfew, at two in the morning. "Time folds."

Time folds in on itself like satin, and there's nothing in-between.

A great blue heron nests in the reeds on the other side of this pond. I watch her often in the mornings, lifting her feet carefully, one by one, moving down the bank, looking for minnows. She came winging home that March afternoon as I sat lost in the memory of my grandfather and I saw her, caught her, in my vision. She flew low, and my awareness of her reflection as it followed her across the water set the years moving again and before long I was recalling myself, nearing forty, sitting in my yellow lawn chair with the frayed bottom, three pages of notes on a legal pad and somewhere to be at seven. The thought made me laugh.

The dogwoods bloom late here in this shaded hollow. But sometimes a red-winged blackbird sings before summer, and the sound can swipe time and carry it out on the pond like a grandfather. There, clear and true, childhood holds, lapping and folding like satin against the sides of a boat, where a girl sits casting a line into the shallows until the blue heron flies, and a woman, laughing on the bank, calls the child home.

FOR THE BEST IN PAPERBACKS, LOOK FOR THE

In every corner of the world, on every subject under the sun, Penguin represents quality and variety—the very best in publishing today.

For complete information about books available from Penguin—including Puffins, Penguin Classics, and Arkana—and how to order them, write to us at the appropriate address below. Please note that for copyright reasons the selection of books varies from country to country.

In the United Kingdom: Please write to *Dept. JC, Penguin Books Ltd, FREEPOST, West Drayton, Middlesex UB7 0BR*.

If you have any difficulty in obtaining a title, please send your order with the correct money, plus ten percent for postage and packaging, to *P.O. Box No. 11, West Drayton, Middlesex UB7 0BR*

In the United States: Please write to *Consumer Sales, Penguin USA, P.O. Box 999, Dept. 17109, Bergenfield, New Jersey 07621-0120*. VISA and MasterCard holders call 1-800-253-6476 to order all Penguin titles

In Canada: Please write to *Penguin Books Canada Ltd, 10 Alcorn Avenue, Suite 300, Toronto, Ontario M4V 3B2*

In Australia: Please write to *Penguin Books Australia Ltd, P.O. Box 257, Ringwood, Victoria 3134*

In New Zealand: Please write to *Penguin Books (NZ) Ltd, Private Bag 102902, North Shore Mail Centre, Auckland 10*

In India: Please write to *Penguin Books India Pvt Ltd, 706 Eros Apartments, 56 Nehru Place, New Delhi 110 019*

In the Netherlands: Please write to *Penguin Books Netherlands bv, Postbus 3507, NL-1001 AH Amsterdam*

In Germany: Please write to *Penguin Books Deutschland GmbH, Metzlerstrasse 26, 60594 Frankfurt am Main*

In Spain: Please write to *Penguin Books S. A., Bravo Murillo 19, 1° B, 28015 Madrid*

In Italy: Please write to *Penguin Italia s.r.l., Via Felice Casati 20, I-20124 Milano*

In France: Please write to *Penguin France S. A., 17 rue Lejeune, F–31000 Toulouse*

In Japan: Please write to *Penguin Books Japan, Ishikiribashi Building, 2–5–4, Suido, Bunkyo-ku, Tokyo 112*

In Greece: Please write to *Penguin Hellas Ltd, Dimocritou 3, GR–106 71 Athens*

In South Africa: Please write to *Longman Penguin Southern Africa (Pty) Ltd, Private Bag X08, Bertsham 2013*